KEEP EVERY LAST DIME

HOW TO AVOID 201
COMMON ESTATE PLANNING
TRAPS AND TAX DISASTERS

BY

RICHARD W. DUFF, J.D., CLU

Published by
RWD Enterprises
Denver

Keep Every Last Dime

How to Avoid 201 Common Estate Planning Traps and Tax Disasters
by Richard W. Duff, J.D., CLU

Published by
RWD Enterprises
1777 South Harrison Street
Denver, Colorado 80210 U.S.A.

www.mcomm.com/duff

Book and cover design by Robert Marcus Graphics, Sebastopol, California
Printed in the United States of America
First Edition, 1998

ISBN 1-882703-00-6

TABLE OF CONTENTS

ACKNOWLEDGEMENTS

Several special ladies contributed their support to this book:

First, I'm truly blessed with the professional editing of Deborah Grandinetti. She is always able to make complex subjects easy to understand. Pamela DuFault, Linda Lund and Laura Miles are tops in their fields of organizing word content and word processing. To Elizabeth Shannon, thank you for stimulating me about how important it is to pay attention to one's personal affairs. Finally, a special thanks to Caryl Lenahan and Catherine Chaffin for those insights that set you apart from other financial planners.

This book doesn't lack for help from men who offered suggestions regarding business and estate planning. Here are a few of them.

Todd Riggs, Clark Harmon, Mike Haizlett and Michael Weinberg made suggestions about various famous people mentioned in this book. Jack Baur, Dick Oshins and Vaughn Henry edited portions for their content. Finally, a special thanks to Bob Allen, Jim Campbell, Tyrone Clark, Rich Elrod, Jay Fifer, Mark Fiore, Rick Haberstroh, Richard Hess, Tom Higgins, Sam Keck, Robert Marcus, Don Milliman, BobRitter, Marv Rothenberg, Mark Trewitt and Dan Wojcik. Fortunately, I paid attention to your advice.

INTRODUCTION

Quick– what do Warren Burger, Jerry Garcia, Estee Lauder and Georgia O'Keefe have in common with Pablo Picasso? Or Jacqueline Onassis for that matter? Or Bob Magness? Can you guess? No? Well, all of these folks amassed a significant personal fortune. They worked hard for it. Unfortunately, they were not spectacularly successful when it came to passing along that fortune—efficiently, without extra taxes or expensive litigation—to the people or organizations that mattered most to them. That meant that a lot of hard-earned dollars went to the government, the lawyers, or both. Surely, that's not what they intended.

I think that's a real shame. And I suspect you feel the same way, too, or else you wouldn't have picked up this book. *Keep Every Last Dime* is for those of you who are committed to careful and creative wealth preservation planning. Maybe that wealth is yours (or your parents), and you want to make sure that the people closest to you get every last dime they can from the estate you've worked so hard to build. (You don't want to see the heirs lose money "to the system" through lack of planning.) Or perhaps you're a financial planner who is committed to helping your clients achieve their goals.

Whether you're a planner, or a well-informed estate owner, you're probably aware that the right strategies can shave off a sizable number of tax dollars from the final estate tax bill, or effectively multiply your money. (For more on that, see my book *Preserving Family Wealth Using Tax Magic: Strategies Worth Millions,* Berkley Books, N.Y., 1995). But did you know that things can still go terribly wrong, even with the best strategies, unless you understand the nuances?

Keep Every Last Dime is a book about the nuances. It's different from every other estate planning book that tells you *how to* set up trusts, wills and family partnerships. This book focuses on *what not to do.* It will help you recognize and avoid the 201 most common estate-planning errors. The book uses plain language to explain these complications, and outlines the most satisfactory solutions. It draws liberally on real-life examples to show what can go wrong when you don't step carefully around these legal and planning "land mines." With estate planning, a little attention to detail can make a major difference in the final result.

If you carefully review your estate plan against the recommendations in *Keep Every Last Dime,* you can rest assured that you have done your very best toward making sure that everything will perform as planned. You'll also have the satisfaction of knowing that the time and money you've invested in the plan have been well spent. With a little luck, the estate will be transferred *as you intended,* without heaping more grief upon your heirs.

Bob Magness, the brilliant founder of Tele-Communications, Inc., inspired this book. If you live in Denver, you may have seen the many newspaper articles in *The Denver Post* and *Rocky Mountain News* on ongoing litigation over the "billion dollar" Magness estate. He died in November

1996, and was a remarkable man in many ways. A pioneer of cable television and modern TV cable systems, to quote *Denver Post* writer Mark Obmascik, he was "smart in life" but "so foolish in death."

I empathize for his wife, Sharon, and his sons, Kim and Gary, who must surely feel that their privacy is violated when the details of estate infighting are splashed across pages of the newspapers. The worst part about all of this is that much of it could have been avoided with some careful planning.

As I read each new article on the Magness estate battle, it occurred to me that perhaps the rest of us could learn from such mistakes. Why repeat the planning errors of others? That's when I set about gathering as many examples as I could, particularly those involving celebrities. You'll find accounts of the successful—or not so successful—estate planning efforts of many luminaries like Marilyn Monroe, Sammy Davis, Jr., Jacqueline Onassis and H.L. Hunt, throughout this book.

WHO THIS BOOK IS FOR

I wrote Every Last Dime for two groups of readers: (1) individuals who have (or will have) sizable estates and (2) professional planners including lawyers, accountants, fund raisers, insurance agents, financial planners and trust officers. You'll also find this book informative if you know that you will be an heir someday, and you have a good enough relationship with your future benefactor to influence the estate planning process.

If you are a successful individual, you'll find this book

useful if:

- You've completed an estate plan and want to check it against what "ought-to-be-done" under most circumstances;
- You are considering a plan and want to learn from the mistakes of others;
- You want to learn the finer points of state-of-the-art planning, in an understandable way; or
- You are curious about how celebrities, who have access to the best estate planning advice money could buy, could trip up here as often as they do.

As a professional planner, you'll find this book interesting if you want:

- Fresh, state-of-the-art information against which to measure your approach to estate planning;
- A checklist of errors and mistakes, and real life examples of disastrous outcomes, to help motivate prospects and clients to do more careful and comprehensive planning; or
- A group of "fall-back" safeguards that will aid you in avoiding malpractice, errors and omissions.

HOW THE BOOK IS ORGANIZED

Chapters 1 and 2 lay out the problems caused by procrastination. The first chapter focuses on personal planning; the second on family businesses. (You'll definitely want to read Chapter 2 if you have a significant share of a company, along with another friend or partner.) You may be very surprised to learn how much good can be accomplished when estate owners are proactive, rather than complacent.

Chapter 3 discusses, the financial aspects of retirement in depth, and explains how inappropriate planning can lead to shockingly heavy taxation of the money set aside in IRAs and qualified retirement plans. People who are knowledgeable enough to make efficient retirement planning choices, may be in a position to reduce estate taxes the "fun" way: by making gifts to family members or worthy causes. In Chapter 4, you'll learn the ins and outs of "gifting." If you have a sincere desire to help others, I'll show you how to avoid the traps that can cause benevolence to "backfire" on you or your beneficiaries. A little know-how can save a lot of money in income, capital gains and estate taxes.

In Chapter 5, you'll learn about the fascinating uses of philanthropy in wealth preservation planning. Unless you know what you're doing, it's easy to trip up here, too, no matter how much you read about this or how noble your intentions to promote the social good.

Chapters 6 and 7 are devoted to tax-deferred annuities and life insurance, respectively. These essential, but misunderstood, financial products can be the source of many problems, if they are poorly arranged in the estate plan. Commercial annuities, for instance, are laden with potential traps. Life insurance (owned by and paid to individuals) seldom confers all the benefits it *could,* if it were better positioned in the overall wealth preservation program. Here you'll learn what it takes to make the best use of your annuity or life insurance contract.

Chapter 8 will give you a working knowledge of the legal

documents that dispose of an estate. Although wills and re-vocable living trusts are the cornerstones to this process, it's easy to miss the opportunities here and end up with an inferior plan. You'll learn how to be proactive and get legal counsel to make provisions for the special needs of your family. As far as I'm concerned, that's the only approach that makes sense.

Chapters 9, 10 and 11 describe life insurance trusts, ex-tended trusts (for the next generation), and perpetual trusts that continue from beneficiary to beneficiary. So many people come up short here and don't take advantage of what's offered by our legal system. You can be the exception. You'll learn why the law truly blesses the wonderful structures we call trusts and how they offer more benefits for you and your family than any other financial strategy.

Each chapter will acquaint you with the benefits of par-ticular planning strategies and the most common mistakes or traps associated with that strategy. You'll also learn what the solutions are. Real-life examples will make the concepts concrete.

I have made every effort to make each chapter as com-plete, and up-to-date as possible. (Just remember that laws can change after a book goes to press.) I sincerely hope you find *Keep Every Last Dime* useful. If you have any comments or suggestions for upcoming editions, I would be delighted to hear from you. In the meantime, I wish you good plan-ning.

Regards,

Dick Duff

AUTHOR'S UPDATE

Bob Magness, founder of Tele-Communications, Inc. (TCI), influenced me to write this book. In 1997, his wife, Sharon, disputed his will, and his sons, Kim and Gary, claimed against her as well. The brothers then sued to remove executors Daniel Ritchie and Donne Fisher, alleging an improper sale of TCI stock.

On Jan. 5, 1998, a settlement was reached in Littleton, Colorado.[1] Reports are that one-half of the TCI stock sale is voided, and TCI must return 16 million shares to the Magness estate. TCI will pay $124 million cash to the estate, $150 million to Chairman John Malone and an undisclosed amount to Sharon Magness. Although one attorney values the settlement at over $300 million, someone must account for the value of the TCI shares (worth $462 million on Jan. 5, 1998) it repaid the estate.

The bottom line: this matter probably cost TCI shareholders (and its subscribers) more than $500 million.

A "message" from Bob Magness:

•   Keep your financial affairs exclusive. Create living trusts for privacy in disability and death.

•   Select a neutral, professional executor.

•   Create documents that discourage disputes.

•   Use life insurance for estate obligations. Surely Magness' premiums would have been under $500 million.

•   Pay closer attention to preserving wealth.

---

1 John Accola and Rebecca Cantwell, "Magness Estate Fight Over," *The Rocky Mountain News,* Jan. 6, 1998, p. B1.

CHAPTER 1

APATHY, TORPOR AND PROCRASTINATION:

THEY'LL GET YOU EVERY TIME

T he late Bob Magness, patriarch of Tele-Communications, Inc.(TCI), the world's largest cable TV empire, was a brilliant, creative man. But his lack of foresight about wealth preservation left experts shaking their heads. A *Rocky Mountain News* staff writer voiced the thoughts of many planning experts when he wrote "...Was it really his intention to hand off more than half his nearly $1 billion fortune to the U.S. government?" Bringing the point home, the writer concluded: "To those who have procrastinated or held off updating wills written years ago: estate planning is a long-term process...(Magness) should have known better."[1]

Having spent fruitless hours in Magness's office in the early 1990s discussing wealth preservation strategies, it is

1 John Accola, "Pitfalls of Poor Planning," *Rocky Mountain News,* Dec. 23, 1996. In late summer of 1997, the State of Colorado announced a tax windfall for fiscal year 1996-97 — and that this was to be refunded somehow to all of its taxpayer-citizens. Now, it appears much of that came in state estate taxes paid by the Magness estate. Aldo Svaldi, "Magness behest: A taxpayer windfall," *The Denver Business Journal,* Oct. 3-9, 1997, p. 1. This really hits home. It's what happens when you must share wealth with a bureaucracy.

frustrating now to watch his estate lawyers and representatives do battle with the IRS, family members – and each other.[2] Magness expended much effort making TCI the best in the field, but he mistakenly assumed that his estate plan would take care of itself. He's not the only one who's made that error.

There seems to be a natural tendency to delay estate planning. Many of us are unwilling to face our own mortality even for the relatively short time it takes to assure the welfare of loved ones. The unfortunate result is that we leave them in a financial mess.[3] The IRS isn't very forgiving, either. Taxes don't diminish just because assets have to be sacrificed to get the tax money. This is a common predicament for heirs whose benefactors fail to plan.

Don't let this happen to you or your loved ones. If you've been procrastinating and feeling guilty about it, this chapter might give you the push you've been needing. I'll describe more than 20 problems that can result from reluctance to get estate planning underway. I'll also outline simple solutions that you can use to avoid these mistakes. Let's start with the biggest one – not starting early enough.

---

2 Mark Obmascik, "A Will With No Way," *The Denver Post,* Sept. 28, 1997, p. 1H. The author wonders how Mr. Magness, acclaimed as a visionary by contemporary Ted Turner, could be "so smart in life"…but "so foolish about death."

3 Even the representatives of CPA Alwin C. Ernst, Senior Account Partner Ernst and Ernst, paid estate costs of $7.1 million ($6.36 million estate taxes — $158,000 cash in the estate) when he died holding a gross estate of $12.6 million. On the other hand, estate taxes on the $53.4 million William Randolph Hearst estate were a mere $3.3 million. Source: 1978 Estate Research Institute.

TWENTY-TWO ESTATE PLANNING GOOFS YOU CAN EASILY AVOID

ERROR #1:

Putting It Off. Does it really make sense to delay estate planning efforts when you're going to eventually transfer the assets anyway, only at a much greater cost (in taxes)? Even worse (like Magness), the money will go to benefit people you'll never meet!

Consider the basic $10,000 annual gift. If you're married, you can gift $20,000 to each child and grandchild (and their spouses). If this is repeated on an annual basis, imagine what can be transferred to family if you begin gifting at age 40.[4] Sam Walton was right when he said, "The best way to reduce paying estate taxes is to give your assets away before they appreciate."[5]

Most people don't feel comfortable making large gifts during peak earning years. Instead, later in life, they sometimes use life insurance to assure completion of the gift-giving plan.

Here's an example: A wealthy couple in their 60s can gift three married children and six grandchildren $240,000 annually over the next 20 years. That is nearly $5 million. Al-

---

4 Some are getting the message. During the 10-year period between 1996-2005, it's estimated that living persons will give their offspring more than $1 trillion (mostly in $10,000 annual gifts) in an effort to reduce estate taxes. This translates to *more than $600,000 per donee.* Thomas J. Stanley and William D. Danko, *The Millionaire Next Door,* Longstreet Press, 1996, pp. 213-214.

5 Sam Walton, *Made in America, My Story,* (Doubleday, 1992).

ternately, they might give an $80,000 annual premium to purchase a $5 million life insurance policy. This enables them to spend other assets, knowing that tax-free gifting is self-completing in event of their deaths.

ERROR #2:

Failing To Plan For An Inheritance. In their study of the estimated $10.4 trillion that baby boomers will inherit, Cornell Professors Avery and Rendall advance three theories to explain bequests: The elderly's need for emergency funds, uncertainty regarding length of life, and an implicit agreement with children to provide care later on.[6] *The problem:* As columnist Andy Zipser tells us, however, most of this wealth will likely be spent before it reaches the children.[7]

My recommendation: Long before a family crisis, prepare for that eventual "reading of the will." Resolve petty differences. Then, call for a family meeting when everyone is healthy. Lay everything on the table in a pleasant and businesslike setting. Are estate documents in place? Is there enough life insurance? Where are important papers and the beneficiary designation forms? Is there room for gifting and philanthropy? Of course, it may be difficult to talk about

---

6 Robert B. Avery and Michael S. Rendall ,*Estimating the Size and Distribution of Baby Boomers' Prospective Inheritances,* Department of Consumer Economics and Housing, Cornell University, Ithaca, NY 14853, 1994.

7 Andy Zipser, "And Now, The Bad News," *Barron's,* Dec. 4, 1995, p. 33.

8 Fearing reprisals and criticism, children often refrain from discussing money with parents until it is too late. It may be that our benefactors are "still in control" because they have the wealth. Or perhaps we feel unworthy when it comes to generosity. Consider author Marianne Williamson's point-of-view as she writes in *Illumi-*

nations, Berkley, 1995, at p. 46. She advises that children shouldn't disdain their natural right to inherit from parents. Simply put, we have an obligation to receive this wealth and pass it on for the benefit of ourselves, our family and community.

money in the family.[8] But it's a whole lot easier to do this when everything is relatively calm.[9]

ERROR #3:

Failing To Admit The Possibility Of Death. It's interesting that most legal and financial counselors don't mention death as a factor in the estate planning process. (Instead, tax savings and avoiding family disputes are probably the keys that motivate clients to take action.)

Nothing can be more wrong. Advisors shouldn't avoid the subject of death. Without admitting this possibility, there is no reason to do anything.

It's been my experience that estate and wealth preservation is a very rewarding experience, when death is discussed openly in the process. For one thing, executing a personal set of documents allows participation in a truly unselfish activity. Think about it. When you sign and make a will out, you're not the one who gains financially. But your loved ones do. Surely you'll feel some peace of mind as you face your mortality, knowing loved ones are provided for.

Estate planning frees energy for lifelong pursuits. It is part of maturing and may even prolong life. As they say, annuitants live longer (just to win a financial "bet" with the insurance company). Why shouldn't those who sign wills live longer, too, knowing their heirs will receive more because

9 According to experts, it's plain common sense for children to maintain a close relationship with potential benefactors. The message is "Call home often and check in with Mom and Dad. Your inheritance may be in the balance." Jerry Morgan, "Family Ties May Affect Inheritance," Newsday as quoted in the *Tribune-Review,* March 20, 1994.

the assets are well-planned?

ERROR #4:

Not Anticipating A Taxable Estate. Nowadays, the stock market is up and so is a 401(k) account. When you add this money (and it's future value) to a home, a life insurance policy and perhaps an inheritance, you just may be wealthier than you think. Don't be surprised if this makes you a candidate for some serious estate planning indeed.[10]

Here's the real issue: Too many people believe that their retirement funds, jointly-owned homes and insurance proceeds can be inherited without placing any tax burden on their heirs. These holdings avoid probate, but this doesn't shelter them from transfer tax concerns. The sad part: Non-probate property probably accounts for most of our net worths. For some reason we still believe IRS only wants an estate tax on probatable assets.

My recommendations: Spend the retirement account. Divide your joint assets with a spouse roughly 50-50; and place the insurance in an irrevocable trust that isn't taxed at either death. It may be necessary, as well, to leave at least $600,000 to an "exemption" trust that misses an estate tax at the death of a spouse.

---

10 By 2005, the number of U.S. millionaire households will reach 5.6 million and nearly 700,000 "millionaires" will leave $2.1 trillion (in 1990 constant dollars) to their heirs between 1996-2005. Thomas J. Stanley and William D. Danko, *The Millionaire Next Door,* Longstreet Press, 1996, p. 212. When life insurance, inflation and other "unclaimed" assets are considered, I believe these numbers are really much larger.

ERROR #5:

Accepting Inferior Advice (When You Don't Have To).
Don't accept anything less than the best financial planning
help you can find. This really doesn't cost any more. Talk
openly with advisors about how much they truly know. For
example, can your accountant value a family business? Can
your lawyer draft a family-bank dynasty trust? Does your
insurance agent truly understand how to position a policy
in the estate plan? Don't rely on "family friends" for guid-
ance just because you've known them over the years. Finally,
get a clear picture in advance about the price. I suggest wealth
preservation is "life's work." It may be that and even more!
The trick is to enjoy this process along the way.

Here's a suggestion for finding the best help. Seek an Ac-
credited Estate Planner (AEP). This is a counselor who has
passed extensive testing by the National Association of Estate Planning Councils. Then determine if he or she has
multiple disciplines. For instance, has a lawyer also been a
trust officer or insurance salesperson? Is a CPA also a CFP,
or ChFC? Is a trust officer educated as a lawyer, too?[11] Seek
to determine whether these advisors work well as a team to

---

11 I'm writing a pamphlet on the qualifications of AEPs, CLUs, CFPs, CPAs, JDs,
MAIs, etc. and how to find them. Contact me for a free copy. Most of these advisors
are bound by professional codes such as the AICPA Professional Standards and the
International Board of Standards and Practices for Certified Financial Planners, the
Codes of Ethics of the National Association of Realtors, Associations of Life Underwriters, The American Society of CLU and ChFC, The Institute of Certified Financial Planners and the International Association of Financial Planners; Model Standards of Practice for Charitable Gift Planners; and the American Bar Association's
Model Rules of Professional Conduct for Lawyers.

do their very best work on your behalf.

My recommendation: When it comes to wealth preservation, be proactive and seek the best advisors. Then ask them to work with those who know you personally. It's always a combination of ability and relationships that works best.

ERROR #6:

Reliance On One Advisor. We often rely on one person to do more than they should. Don't ask a lawyer for advice on life insurance matters. Don't expect an accountant to handle investments, too. And don't make an insurance agent ask the company to prepare a legal document. It's just not wise to rely on any one person for too much advice. Nor is it professional for one advisor to assume tasks outside his or her training, licensing or expertise.

My recommendation: Don't ask for too much, but expect an expert to always give top-notch information — and if one member of your team can't pull their weight, get a replacement. A team should share talents; and they should be compensated fairly and well for their skills. Keep in mind that "we really do get what we pay for," when it comes to estate planning.

ERROR #7:

Poor Accounting - Loans To Children. Let's suppose you advance Mark $100,000 to make a down payment on a residence. Or you give Heather $50,000 to go to medical school. Are these loans? Or are they gifts where children don't even make payments of the interest?

I know a father who "loaned" three children $850,000 in unequal amounts. He juggled his "books," and made decisions whenever payments were missed. His financial statement didn't list these "loans" as receivables, and frankly he doesn't have a clue as to what he is doing. Worse yet: His children don't either.

Someday, the family will pay an estate tax on these "loans." Then, there will probably be a family squabble as well when one child learns that he or she has been "shortchanged."

My recommendation: Decide now whether an advancement is a loan or a gift. Treat each child fairly and equally. Get the matter resolved just as soon as possible. Then, purchase life insurance to bring each child to an equal amount when all loans are considered.

ERROR #8:

Not Acquiring Long-Term Care (LTC) Insurance At An Early Date. Presently, most LTC insurance provides benefits in the nursing home or at home. Policies usually provide coverage if the insured cannot perform the activities of daily living (ADLs) without help. And insurance companies offer "early" coverage, at guaranteed renewable premiums, for people in their 40s and 50s.

The question isn't whether this insurance is affordable. Individuals who have the good sense to purchase LTC insurance won't have to liquidate capital someday for what costs pennies on the dollar today. Remember, there is no way to know what it will cost to obtain quality health care as one advances in age.

If the annual premium for a $100 daily lifetime benefit costs $1,000 when you're in your 50s, it will likely double in your 60s and may double again in your 70s. In your 80s, coverage may not even be available due to poor health. That's why I recommend buying an LTC policy today. Select one that holds its premium and entitles you to automatic improvements and updates as the years ago by!

ERROR #9:

Not Keeping Good Records. Neglecting to keep files for each investment, insurance policy and document, can be costly for your heirs. When your children are sorting through file folders and piles of canceled checks, they may overlook many important papers and records. They may even think a valuable investment or antique is just old and worthless.

That's why it's important to list and update investments at least annually. List current values and attach supporting documents to establish basis for income taxes. Keep a file folder for each life insurance policy and include an in-force ledger that indicates current and projected policy values. Ask an insurance counselor to furnish this information each year.

Also keep a file that shows the credit life insurance and accidental death coverage provided by your bank from time to time. Include with these records any miscellaneous coverage such as cancer or loss of limb insurance.

This way, when the day comes to go through your important records, it will take your children two or three hours at most and be relatively painless. Your children will certainly appreciate this thoughtfulness.

ERROR #10:

Believing Congress Will "Fix" The Estate Tax. Through the years, there have been frequent proposals to eliminate the estate tax.[12] Others argue that it should be maintained just to redistribute the wealth.[13]

Who is right? It's hard to say, but let's hope for the best — and expect the worst. It is unlikely, however, that we'll see transfer taxes completely eliminated.[14] And things can get worse. For openers, if Treasury has its way, the $10,000 gift tax exclusion will become more restrictive. Valuation discounts for minority interests and lack of marketability will be reduced, also, and there will be a capital gains tax at death on the appreciation in investments. Charitable remainder trusts won't be the same, and it won't be possible to place life insurance in an irrevocable trust.

---

12 Newt Gingrich, "End These Senseless Taxes," *USA Today,* April 14, 1997, p. 14A.

13 "Gingrich Proposes Gift: Tax Cuts for the Well-Off," *USA Today,* p. 14A, April 14, 1997. As Congress revamps the IRS in 1997, columnists still argue that our unfair Tax Code is best for the country. See Cokie and Steven V. Roberts, "Complex or Not, The Tax Code Has Served It's Ends," United Feature Syndicate, *The Rocky Mountain News,* Oct. 19, 1997, p. 3B.

14 See Jane Bryant Quinn, "Forget Tax Cuts, Work On The Deficit," in *Staying Ahead, a feature of The Rocky Mountain News,* Aug. 4, 1997, p. 2B. Ms. Quinn takes the position that there are no economic reasons to cut capital gains taxes or estate taxes. She argues that all tax cuts should be "canned," and we should put this revenue toward budget balance. Although the Taxpayers Relief Act of 1997 gradually increases the $600,000 "exemption" to $1 million (see Exhibit 1 at the end of this chapter), I simply use $600,000 throughout this book.

For these reasons, do your planning now, and establish flexible legal and financial structures that are grandfathered under the law. Include "trap door" features also (for example, see Chapter 9, Mistake # 3) that allow advisors to adapt to laws that surely will change over the years.

ERROR #11:

Not Providing "Opportunities" For Children. Gifts to others are taxable transfers, with the following exceptions: Annual $10,000 gift exclusions and gifts that pay medical and education expenses. If you wish to "create" value for a child, however, the law permits you to provide benefits in other ways without creating a taxable transfer. Build a home, for instance, and let an heir occupy it rent-free. Ask well-placed friends, or use your influence in the community, to help children obtain loans at favorable rates. Share your own knowledge and help descendants build their business and social relationships. None of these gifts are considered taxable transfers. In short, instead of focusing solely on building an estate tax base, help children create wealth themselves. Then, they'll already own it.

ERROR #12:

Forgetting Advisors' Admonitions. If planning is "cutting-edge," something can always go wrong. For example, when advisors create a "state-of-the-art" wealth preservation plan, they'll probably suggest special gifting discounts, that are always subject to audit by IRS. A lawyer will caution you that this possibility exists, and it will be easy to miss this warning during the planning process. If you are admonished to keep especially good records, follow this advice. It will pay dividends later.

Also be aware that when a lawyer completes the plan, he or she may "sign-off" on liability for future estate problems. Although it's best to have on-going dialogue instead, it is proper for an attorney to make it clear that liability stops when the plan is completed.[15]

ERROR #13:

Not Planning For A Failed Marriage. In our society, it appears that a marriage has a greater than 50 percent chance of failure. And the richer you are, the more it costs when divorce papers are filed.[16]

Revlon billionaire Ronald Perelman paid $8 million to divorce his first wife, Faith, and $80 million to divorce his second wife, Claudia. Wiser for these experiences, he'll apparently pay less to divorce a third wife, Patricia.[17]

And you've probably heard about the divorce case of *Wendt v. Wendt*. After Lorna Wendt turned down $10 million, she

---

15 It's important to understand an attorney's dilemma when the estate plan is finally completed. Is he or she required to alert you to changes in the law as they occur? Or is it the client's responsibility to pay attention and schedule the next appointment when appropriate? I recommend that you discuss these issues with your lawyer at the beginning of the relationship.

16On the other hand, if you have money it may be easier to stay married — and just "start" another family. According to the *Texas Monthly*, April of 1978, multi-billionaire H.L. Hunt had three separate simultaneous "families" as he built his fortune. And his heirs were chagrined at the "shoddy legal form of his will" (and perhaps his estate plan) which had no provisions for charity or avoiding taxes either.

17 Brigid McMenamin, in "'Til Divorce Do Us Part," *Forbes,* Ocober, 14, 1996.

sought about $50 million. She argues that she deserves it because she raised the children, and was a dutiful homemaker and corporate wife.[18]

To avoid problems like this, consider obtaining an offshore trust before marriage. Create a family partnership and a revocable trust when the seas are calm. If there is danger from a lawsuit (including a divorce someday), a foreign trustee takes title to property and keeps everyone at bay until matters are settled. My favorite asset protection specialist is a personal friend- Barry Engel, Esq. You can reach him at Engel, Reiman & Lockwood, in Englewood, Colorado. He'll work well with personal counsel in your state.

If you haven't done this kind of planning and the possibility of divorce creeps into the marriage insidiously, here are items to address before matters get more serious:

· Ask family to hold off making gifts to you. If a donor must make transfers for personal estate planning reasons, ask him or her to place assets in a separate spendthrift trust for your benefit. (Since this property still may not be sheltered from upcoming support obligations, have the trust give a friend discretion to make payments on your behalf.)

· If you've previously divided assets with a spouse for asset protection purposes, attempt to establish that these transfers are for convenience and are not completed gifts.

· Review agreements that may require the sale of a busi-

---

18 Dobrynski, "Divorce Executive Style, Revisited," *New York Times,* Jan., 1997. Although in Nov., 1997, a judge finally awarded her about $20 million, I somehow don't feel this case is over.

ness interest to co-investors, in the event of a divorce. If these terms exist, it may be possible to make alternative arrangements now to protect against unintended loss if the marital rift gets more serious.

· Review your will immediately. If it leaves everything to the spouse you are about to divorce, consider changing this to no more than the minimum ⅓ or ½ right of election share required under state law.

ERROR #14:

No Asset Protection Plan. It seems that people are willing to sue over just about anything these days. If you've got significant assets, you've got a right to be concerned. Fortunately, there are strategies you can implement now to protect you later. They only work if you implement them before there's even a hint of trouble. Otherwise, you could be charged with trying to hinder, delay or defraud a potential creditor.

Here are eight such strategies, starting with the simplest and progressing to the most comprehensive.

A. A quality liability insurance program. The most basic plan is an umbrella policy providing minimum benefits, and the most comprehensive approach is errors and omissions or malpractice coverage for professional persons. Unfortunately, a lawsuit typically alleges more serious charges that aren't covered by the insurance.

B. Your home and other assets that are exempt from attachment under state law. Indeed, in some states like Florida, it may be possible to safeguard some serious money in an expensive residence that is fully protected under the law. Keep in mind, however, that it's necessary to acquire an exempt asset before a financial crisis begins. And it's always possible that the law granting the shelter will change at a moment's notice.

C. Cash values in life insurance and annuity policies. As a general rule, expect one-half of all states to fully protect insurance policies from creditors (and the remainder to provide at least some coverage). Only about 30 states exempt annuity values and the coverage is usually limited to a portion of the policy's value. Ask your insurance agent for more information. You may be surprised how much the law shelters cash money when it reappears inside a life insurance or annuity contract.

D. Irrevocable trusts (ILITs) for family members. If life insurance is acquired in an ILIT for the benefit of family members other than the insured, the trust can express a creator's intention to protect trust assets from creditors of trust beneficiaries. Since cash values already have statutory protection, the trust now adds an additional layer of shelter for your heirs. By using "trap doors" (see Chapter 9), it may even be possible to provide the insured some indirect access to trust assets in emergencies.

E. An Alaskan trust. Lawyer Jonathan Blattmachr has apparently drafted laws allowing a trust located in Alaska to permit an independent trustee to distribute funds to the trust creator. Trust assets are sheltered from a grantor's creditors, and advocates claim estate tax advantages as well. These trusts aren't yet proven in the law, and I recommend caution before you create one as a cornerstone to an asset protection plan.

F.   Corporations, limited liability companies and family limited partnerships. These business entities offer shareholders and owners an increased layer of creditor protection. There are a few problems, however. Don't expect these structures to protect your outside personal property from those making claims against you. Secondly, you will probably need an actual business (under state law) before its assets can be safeguarded in the entity. Finally, keep in mind that lawyers are especially creative when they seek assets from a defendant. While business entities offer considerable protection, do not expect them to fully shelter everything they (or you) own.

G.   Trusts created by others for you. Our law blesses trust funds created to benefit loved ones. (See Chapters 8, 9, 10, and 11.) Whenever a benefactor wants to help you financially, ask that the gift or bequest be placed in a trust fund for your benefit. Have a lawyer protect trust assets if you incur legal threats to your financial situation. It's simply remarkable how much a trust creator can do by placing funds in a trust to help others.

H.   Offshore or foreign trusts. Those really serious minded about forestalling future claims against them will establish a foreign trust for their personal property. These structures do not claim income gift or estate tax savings. Rather, an offshore trust is carefully established where the law is just not friendly to creditors of local citizens and people from other countries such as the United States. The creator's assets are then placed out of the U.S. or remain stateside until there is a need to shift them out of the country. You'll need an excellent international lawyer to insure the success of this strategy.

The important thing is to create your asset protection plan in advance. It won't do you much good to draft a meticulous estate plan if someone is just going to gobble up those assets in the meantime. Why leave yourself open to the possibility?

ERROR #15:

Believing A Spouse Will Spend Everything After Your Death. Since 1982, there has been an unlimited marital deduction that defers payment of estate taxes until the second spouse dies. You may believe that your spouse will just liquidate everything after you die, but it's more likely that he or she will spend less instead of more.

My recommendation: Use a strategy that actually encourages a "spend down" approach like a private annuity where a spouse sells her inheritance to children for a lifetime annuity income. If he or she dies, payments cease and there is no estate tax (since there is nothing left to transfer). Sure, it can be a problem if your spouse gives up access to principal in exchange for the annuity income. Nonetheless, a private annuity makes perfectly good sense in situations where he or she has a diminished (but not terminal) life expectancy.

ERROR #16:

Owning "Too Much" Of One Asset. Sometimes, it's not
best to own "too much of a good thing." For example, when
William Paley died in 1989, his family received an 8 percent
stake in CBS - 1.9 million shares valued at nearly $300 mil-
lion. Mr. Paley's executors wanted to sell this block because
his estate had to raise over $190 million to "cover tax obliga-
tions." Because of its size, they had difficulty finding the
right buyer.[19]

But you don't have to be a Forbes 400 family, to suffer
from the effects of holding a large block of securities. The
ranks of family-owned and operated newspapers are shrinking rapidly, according to Ruth Lehman, matriarch of several
Colorado newspapers. She finds it sad when families can't
continue the tradition because of estate taxes.[20]

My recommendation: Diversify holdings and arrange es-

19 See Dennis Keale, "Paley's CBS Stake May Have To Be Sold, Raising Prospect of
Speculation in Stock," *The Wall Street Journal,* Nov. 7, 1990. Mr. Keale points out
that CBS was especially vulnerable to an unfriendly takeover. Imagine what happens when a large block of stock in any business is sold by an estate. First the buyer
is fully aware of the circumstances leading to a transaction where "top dollar" is not
offered. Secondly, the sale is never at the right time; after all perhaps the driving
force behind the company has just passed away. Finally, a new buyer is in an excellent position to take control of the company and "oust" key officers previously in-
charge. These were exactly the issues faced by the estate of Bob Magness when it
made a stock deal with TCI Chairman John Malone, Merrill Lynch and Lehman
Bros. to get the estate tax money. See John Accola , "TCI Gets Help On Magness
Tax Bill," *Rocky Mountain News,* June 18, 1997. Predictably, the Magness sons are
suing the estate's executors alleging this $529 million stock deal was underhanded
and inappropriate. Stephen Keating, "Estate Feud May Take Years," *The Denver
Post,* Sept. 17, 1997, p. C1.

20 Ellen Miller, "Publisher Confirms Sale of Montrose Daily Press," *The Denver
Post,* Feb. 7, 1997.

tate liquidity. To get full value, consider selling a block of stock, early on, when there isn't any apparent reason for the sale.

ERROR #17:

Holding Too Many Illiquid Assets. Nowadays, it doesn't seem worth it to stash significant amounts of personal cash in the bank. There are just too many exciting investment opportunities competing for these dollars. But usually the greater an investment reward, the more difficult it is to liquidate the asset in an emergency.[21] This causes an illiquid and unwieldy situation for an estate.

Lack of liquidity is a severe problem, especially when it comes to paying estate taxes nine months after death.[22] Es-

---

21 According to William O. Donoghue, in "Money Wise," Tribune Media Services, Inc., *The Denver Post,* Oct. 25, 1992, Allovise, the wife of Sammy Davis, Jr., held a massive auction to sell valuable family heirlooms to pay IRS $5.2 million in estate taxes. What a shame if his family lost a platinum record collection with the slam of an auctioneer's hammer. It's also reported that the four great-great-great granddaughters of John Audobon may have sold their ancestor's rare artwork just to pay "crushing inheritance taxes." See Eric Gregory, "Tax Bill Imperils Art Collections," *The Atlanta Constitution,* Feb. 10, 1993, p. A3.

22 Consider for example the sad story of the Joe Robbie children who had to sell a controlling interest in the Miami Dolphins. As reported in "Robbie Tax Bill May Force Sale of Dolphin Stake," *The Miami Herald,* Jan. 10, 1992, p. 1C, the sale of the Dolphins was a likely probability unless they could find some money (to pay taxes). According to "Robbie's Agree to Sell a Majority Interest in the Dolphins," *Wall Street Journal,* June 16, 1993, there finally was a deal that included Joe Robbie Stadium consummated with H. Wayne Huizinga, the chief executive of Blockbuster Entertainment.

23 According to Mike Freeman, "New Goal for Giants Owner: Hold That Team," *The New York Times,* Nov. 19, 1995, several NFL teams are vulnerable to sale because of inevitable estate tax burdens. For instance, apparently one of the reasons Art Modell moved the Cleveland Browns was because Baltimore gave him a reported $50 million bonus to relocate. (Mr. Modell wanted this money to pay some

tate advisors are always concerned about doing battle with IRS where there isn't any bargaining room or enough money to settle a tax dispute.[23]

My recommendation: Make a tax liquidity plan now. Buy life insurance. A policy with a quality carrier provides the assurance that your family won't be at the mercy of an unfriendly system, and better yet, it will cost you only a fraction of what it could cost your estate later if you don't take this step.[24] Step back and take a moment to assess any lack of liquidity in your situation. Then obtain a first rate policy at a young age when you're in the best of health. You won't regret this and neither will the family.

ERROR #18:

Holding Everything In Joint Tenancy To Avoid Probate. For some reason, America has a "love affair" with joint tenancy (with right of survivorship) property titling. However, joint tenancy can create special problems at death because this property passes directly to a surviving joint tenant.

---

of the estate tax.) Imagine what some creative estate and insurance planning might do in situations like this! A collar may be the solution when there is a lack of estate liquidity. (See the first footnote of Chapter 5.) Indeed, the Magness family will surely make this point against executors who sold TCI stock to pay estate taxes. See Stephen Keating, "Magness Versus Magness," *Denver Post,* Nov. 16, 1997, P. 1A. Keep in mind that collars involve conservative securities options transactions that require specialized assistance. I recommend that you contact Jim Campbell of the Denver Paine Webber office for more information about them.

24 Damel Duncrief, "Don't Get Blindsided," *Financial Planning,* March, 1994, referring to a quote by Richard Mahmarian that $45 million in Robbie estate taxes could have been paid with *a life insurance check.* It would have certainly improved the financial composition of a family situation. He infers that there are a lot of people who do what they do best; however, they just neglect other areas of their financial life.

Even though a will leaves "everything in trust," a will doesn't dispose of joint property. The result: A spouse's inheritance is made fully available to estate taxes, judgment creditors and possibly a new paramour.

From an estate tax point-of-view, too much joint tenancy also "over-qualifies" a marital deduction. In other words, an estate may miss a $600,000 "exemption" trust that bypasses taxes at a spouse's death. In addition, only one-half of assets held jointly receive a basis step-up at death. If this property is, say, an apartment house, then only 50 percent receives a current market value basis and a new depreciation schedule.

My recommendation: Divide joint tenancy assets prior to death. Then, create "exemption" trusts that receive up to $600,000 at the first death. You'll save estate taxes, and there won't be a depreciation schedule where one-half of an asset has a basis step-up and the other one-half doesn't.

ERROR #19:

Not Splitting Assets With Your Spouse. Even though you own property in your personal names - and not in joint tenancy-it's still possible to "over-qualify" the marital deduction by not taking advantage of the $600,000 bypass "exemption" trust.[25]

---

25 According to the Associated Press, "Ex-Justice Leaves a Slapdash Will," *The Denver Post,* Nov. 1, 1995, even Warren Burger, once the nation's highest ranking judge didn't do a very good job of arranging assets with his spouse, either. Aside from a number of drafting errors and misspellings in his handwritten will, the article infers when his wife, Virginia, predeceased him that she didn't leave a $600,000 "exemption" trust. The result: His family paid federal and estate taxes of over $450,000, and he possibly could have saved his family this expense.

Let's say you and your wife own property worth $2 million. It is all in your name, and a will leaves everything to her in a marital deduction trust. The full $2 million is taxed in her subsequent estate where the family loses benefit of your $600,000 "exemption." Here is the result: Your descendants pay an estate tax of $588,000 instead of merely $320,000.

My recommendation: Retitle approximately $1 million in each name. Then, make a $600,000 family by-pass trust available for the survivor no matter who dies first. (See Illustration #1.)

ERROR #20:

Not Obtaining Separate Counsel For Spouses In Second Marriages. In a first marriage, each spouse probably has similar estate planning goals and objectives. One law firm does everything. Each parent leaves a $600,000 family by-pass trust at the first death. The remaining assets pass to a marital deduction QTIP trust. Finally, everything is divided into shares for children at the second death.

But planning changes when there is a second or third marriage, and children from previous relationships. Let's say your sons and daughters tend to be older, as a group, than your spouse's children. (Perhaps your spouse is closer to their age.) You are the wealthier spouse, and there is a prenuptial agreement that looms as an issue. If you leave assets to your spouse, he or she may even disinherit your children. And don't forget the premarital agreement that is legally binding

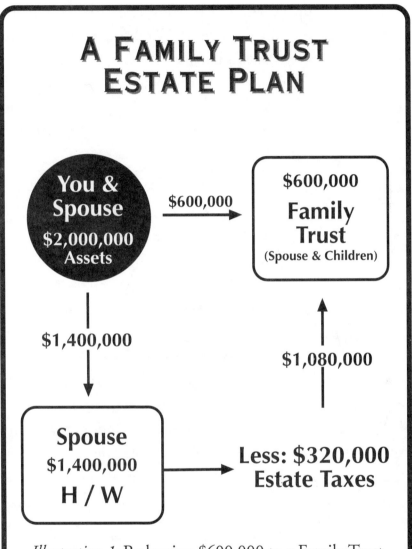

Illustration 1: By leaving $600,000 to a Family Trust, which children receive tax-free at the second death, you and your spouse obtain *two* $600,000 "exemptions" for your estates. Instead of paying $588,000, your children owe merely $320,000 in estate taxes– *a savings of $268,000!*

unless it is changed. These factors and others can create some real conflicts of interest when the family goals are different.

My recommendation: Obtain individual legal counsel. Then have these separate attorneys combine their talents to fulfill your wishes. This will forestall a likely dispute between children and step-or adopted children within the extended family.[26]

ERROR #21:

Not Considering U.S. Tax Law Affecting A Foreign Spouse. More than once, I've reviewed estate planning papers that aren't appropriate because only one spouse is a U.S. citizen. It just seems that financial and legal counselors don't understand how serious this matter is.[27]

Let's say one spouse is a citizen of Canada (who lives here as a resident alien). In this circumstance, the U.S. government is concerned that he or she may inherit from a U.S. citizen and move marital trust assets out of the country. Therefore, in order to ensure collection of estate tax at the second death, this trust must be a qualified domestic trust (a QDOT). A QDOT requires one trustee who is a U.S. citizen. It withholds estate taxes on most distributions to a sur-

---

26 Although it's possible to employ only one attorney when it comes to spouse-spouse, parent-child and partner-partner planning, it may be much better to choose individual counselors. Consider the ethical dilemmas when, for example, one spouse tells a "mutual" lawyer about a personal "secret" and then asks the attorney to withhold this information from a mate.

27 Mary Rowland, "Out of reach non-citizens with substantial assets can pay heavy price in estate taxes," New York Times News Services, *The Chicago Tribune,* Oct. 18, 1994. She correctly points out one of the biggest mistakes by estate planning professionals is their failure to consider clients' citizenship.

viving mate. (The trust pays an estate tax, also, on assets remaining at the surviving spouse's death.)

There are also additional requirements that lawyers must include in a QDOT. Here's the point: Advisors should always ask about citizenship. This can avert an unexpected tax bill at the first death.[28]

ERROR #22:

Not Having A Review Procedure. I believe that most errors can be prevented if you (a) start early on, (b) have competent advisors, and (c) encourage a systematic review.

If advisors do a "one-time" estate plan, they will be only too careful to sign-off on future matters beyond their control. On the other hand, a quality wealth preservation team should agree on follow-up meetings at least every year, and when there are changing circumstances such as death, illness, or divorce in the family.

After all, it's possible to overlook something in the early years if everyone is just getting acquainted. When matters are reviewed regularly, it's possible to use checks and balances to determine if the plan is working. You'll find, also, that when next year's appointment is set, the advisors take a personal interest in keeping each other up-to-date on changes

---

28 See also, Robert Lenzner and Philippe Mao, "The new refugees," *Forbes,* Nov. 21, 1994. The authors explain that some prominent persons are choosing to forego U.S. citizenship by expatriating to another country. Expatriates in the early 90s include Michael Dingman, a Ford Motor director (to the Bahamas); John Dorrance, an heir to the Campbell Soup fortune (to Ireland); and Kenneth Dart, an heir to Dart Container (to Belize). These persons, and their spouses, need especially creative legal counsel to assure legitimate avoidance of the U.S. transfer tax system.

that should be made.

In the next chapter, we'll look at how to avoid common errors in family business succession planning. Taking care here can prevent your family business from being among the two-thirds that don't survive as a second-generation family business.

EXHIBIT 1

REDUCTION IN ESTATE TAX
FROM INCREASED UNIFIED CREDIT *

Taxable Estate	1998	1999	Death Occurring in Year 2000 or 2001	2002 or 2003	2004	2005	2008 & Thereafter
$ 625,000	$9,250	$ 9,250	$ 9,250	$29,250	$ 9,250	$ 9,250	$ 9,250
$ 650,000	$9,250	$18,500	$18,500	$18,500	$18,500	$ 18,500	$ 18,500
$ 675,000	$9,250	$18,500	$27,750	$27,750	$27,750	$ 27,500	$ 27,750
$ 700,000	$9,250	$18,500	$27,750	$37,000	$37,000	$ 37,000	$ 37,000
$ 725,000	$9,250	$18,500	$27,750	$37,000	$46,250	$ 46,250	$ 46,250
$ 750,000	$9,250	$18,500	$27,750	$37,000	$55,500	$ 55,500	$ 55,500
$ 775,000	$9,250	$18,500	$27,750	$37,000	$65,250	$ 65,250	$ 65,250
$ 800,000	$9,250	$18,500	$27,750	$37,000	$75,000	$ 75,000	$ 75,000
$ 825,000	$9,250	$18,500	$27,750	$37,000	$84,750	$ 84,750	$ 84,750
$ 850,000	$9,250	$18,500	$27,750	$37,000	$94,500	$ 94,500	$ 94,500
$ 875,000	$9,250	$18,500	$27,750	$37,000	$94,500	$104,250	$104,250
$ 900,000	$9,250	$18,500	$27,750	$37,000	$94,500	$114,000	$114,000
$ 925,000	$9,250	$18,500	$27,750	$37,000	$94,500	$123,750	$123,750
$ 950,000	$9,250	$18,500	$27,750	$37,000	$94,500	$133,500	$133,500
$ 975,000	$9,250	$18,500	$27,750	$37,000	$94,500	$133,500	$143,250
$1,000,000*	$9,250	$18,500	$27,750	$37,000	$94,500	$133,500	$153,000

*For example, if death occurs in 1998, the $600,000 "Exemption" is $625,000—in 2003, it is $700,000; and in 2008, it is $1 million. This chart assumes the estate does not qualify for the Family Owned Business Exclusion under Section 2033A of the Code and that unified credit has not been used for lifetime gifts.

CHAPTER 2

FAMILY BUSINESS SUCCESSION PLANNING:
AN AMERICAN TRAGEDY

Seventy-five to ninety-five percent of all U.S. companies are family-owned, so it's likely that you or a family member own or work for one of these companies. Unfortunately, because of inadequate planning, only *one-third* [1] of all family businesses survive to the second generation, and a mere *one-eighth* make it to the third generation. Just imagine that - the life's work of so many people destroyed! We've all heard the expression, "We don't plan to fail; we just fail to plan." Take heart! There is a better way!

In this chapter, I'll tell you why so many family businesses fail and how proper planning can ensure their survival. I'll also outline several problems associated with tax and life insurance strategies, and show you useful ways to save money and reduce taxes when you do business and financial planning. As you read, keep in mind that family business planning requires you to pay close attention to de-

---

1 Edward F. Koren, Esq., and Marc A. Silverman, Ph.D., *Family Business Succession Planning,* a paper presented at the 1997 Phillip P. Heckerling Miami Estate Planning Institute.

tails and relationships. If it's going to work, the founder, heirs, and the legal and financial advisors have to stay in close communication.

WHY BUSINESSES FAIL

ERROR # 1:

Operating With No Business Continuation Plan. Why is it that only 33 percent of all family businesses succeed past the first generation? It isn't always just the death of a founder. In one survey[2] in which heirs were interviewed, most said the primary causes of business failure were financially-oriented. Here were the top five problems:

1. 99 percent surveyed attributed the failure to the fact that the founder didn't have an adequate estate plan;

2. 98 percent said that there wasn't enough money to pay the estate tax;

3. 97 percent said that the founder didn't prepare to transfer the business;

4. 90 percent said that there were conflicts with nonactive family members; and

5. 86 percent said that the founder's advisors didn't perform adequately.[3]

---

2 Russ Alan Prince and Karen Maru File, "Marketing to Family Business Owners," *The National Underwriter*, 1995, Chapter 2, at page 35, where results of 479 family interviews are summarized. There is another study sponsored by National of Vermont which examines 749 family businesses that failed within four years after being transferred to the second generation. Over 97 percent of these inheritors blamed the founders for being negligent in not having an adequate estate plan or preparing for a business transition.

---

3 It's interesting that 411 (86 percent) of 479 family descendant groups indicated

From my experience, it seems that many successful entrepreneurs are so busy making money that they frequently don't "stop and smell the roses," as the saying goes. It's just so much easier to defer planning until another day.

But this can blow everything up in a heartbeat. Consider the family business owner who refused to discuss a business continuation plan with his two sons. He told them: "I'm never going to retire; you can solve the problems when I'm dead." One day, on an out-of-town business trip, the sons "kidnapped" their father. They told him their private plane wouldn't take him home until he prepared a succession plan. Then, the plane flew to the home of a planning consultant who was waiting to help them begin the process.[4]

My recommendation: Successor planning is a lifelong process. The moment you get involved in a business, begin working on an exit strategy. In fact, the instant that you start to "relax" is precisely the moment to begin developing a business perpetuation plan.[5]

---

that the founder's advisors didn't stack-up"; incidentally, only 9 percent admitted *their* advisors performed inadequately.

4 Craig E. Aronoff, Ph.D., and John L. Ward, Ph.D., *Family Business Succession: The Final Test of Greatness* (Business Owner Resources, Marietta, GA.), for their interesting perspective on family business succession planning.

5 Matthew Schifrin and Sharon Moshavi, "Don't let your family fight over family conflicts," a sidebar of "When Heirs Fall Out," *Forbes,* Dec. 6, 1993, pp. 140-143. The authors suggest that business owners should always have a well-conceived exit strategy. There are several interesting situations detailed, including the "squabbling" families of William Dart (Dart Container Corp.); Herbert Haft (Dart Group); Joseph Gallo (Gallo Wine); and William, Charles and David Koch (Koch Industries). Each involves the most bitter sibling rivalry, family feuding and legal skullduggery imaginable.

Here is a 13-question checklist (based on suggestions by Messrs. Koren and Silverman[6] in their paper on Family Business Succession Planning) to help you make a quick review of your own family business. It will remind you to initiate a discussion with legal and financial advisors about a continuity plan.

1. Is there trust there between parents and active children? Or among the active children themselves?

2. Is there good communication between active and inactive children?

3. Do family members tend to have high self-esteem?

4. Are differences in the family well-accepted?

5. Is there good humor, openness and respect in the family, or is there mostly sarcasm, secrecy and suspicion?

6. Are business decisions made for business reasons? In other words, is it "just business" and "nothing personal?"

7. Does "win-win" take over when there are family conflicts?

8. Are problems solved by a team approach, rather than unilaterally?

9. Are family members (active and inactive) specifically acknowledged, appreciated and rewarded for their accomplishments?

10. Are all family members free from chemical dependency, alcoholism or stress-related difficulties?

11. Are feelings of hurt and anger dealt with fairly and with compassion?

6 *Supra*, note 1.

12. Is there a tendency to accept blame for mistakes and trip-ups?

13. Is there a well-functioning Board of Directors consisting at least partly of non- family members?

My recommendation: If most of your answers are no, take the advice of Koren and Silverman and see a family business consultant. It's probably time to have a business succession checkup.

ERROR # 2:

Operating With An Inadequate Business Succession Plan. Having any old plan isn't necessarily a wise move, especially if the founder unilaterally chooses a successor in power.

Take the situation of George Berkowitz, originator of Legal Sea Foods. According to Koren and Silverman,[7] Mr. Berkowitz chose his oldest son to succeed him in power, so the middle son promptly left the business to open a competitive restaurant. Family dynamics were changed forever because Mr. Berkowitz acted without consulting anyone.

Family problems also beset the family of the late Robert Irsay, former owner of the Indianapolis Colts football team.[8] Despite the fact that an allegedly-binding divorce agreement transfers ownership of the franchise to Bob's son, Jim[9]; the heirs are still involved in a spirited squabble over the Irsay

7 *Supra,* note 1.

8 Dick Cady, "The Irsay Saga: money, hard feelings and a team in limbo," *The Indianapolis Star,* Nov. 24, 1996, p. 1.

9 Mike Chappell, "Operation of Colts will stay in family," *The Indianapolis Star,* Jan. 16, 1997.

empire.[10] Stay tuned.

A good succession plan can prevent problems like these. According to authors Aronoff and Ward,[11] the key elements to a good succession plan include:

1. A family mission statement prepared with the input of family members, that articulates a commitment to continue the business as a family-owned enterprise.

2. The instillation of family values and a work ethic in children when they are young.

3. The common sense to allow successor candidates to work outside the business during their 20s.

4. The foresight to choose the likely successor (or successors) in his or her 30s, and try the successor(s) out by assigning them to run an important area of the business before taking over the entire operation.

5. The wisdom to choose a successor candidate based on something more tangible than his or her position as a "favorite" child. Instead, communicate carefully that the successor-to-be is chosen because of meeting independent criteria. (Perhaps this should be determined by an outside Board of Directors.)

6. The maturity to let the successor establish a personal identity and style, instead of imitating the founder.

7. The grace to pass the baton to the successor without grudges or reluctance.

---

10 Dick Cady, "More secrets of the Irsays might be aired in estate fight," *The Indianapolis Star*, Feb. 2, 1977.

11 *Supra*, note 4.

8. And the discipline to keep estate and business plans up-to-date and in line with the succession plan.[12]

ERROR # 3:

Treating Active And Inactive Children Unequally. Just because you've chosen a successor, the transfer of corporate control may be quite a different matter. Although a good business succession plan probably involves a shift of power while you are alive, in many situations, founders keep voting control until they die. Then it becomes important to treat active and inactive children *equally* when it's time to divide up family assets.

Let's say you and your wife, Barbara, are company creators. Your children are Andy, who is active, and Becky, who is inactive. You have a business that currently appraises for $2 million, and there is an insurance policy that pays estate taxes at the second death. You want to give the business to Andy, but treat both children fairly and equally. Here are a few ideas on how to accomplish this when Barbara and you are gone:

· Bequeath the business to Andy and acquire life insurance to equalize things for Becky. If the business doesn't appraise for $2 million, either Andy and Becky can make a financial adjustment between them, or you can decide to

---

12 Another key tendency in planning is to overcomplicate everything. According to Charles V. Bagli, "The New York Report," *The New York Times,* April 10, 1997; Harry Helmsley, who died in January of 1997, did exactly that. Mr. Helmsley's wife, Leona, is involved in several lawsuits to unravel the many partnerships that Harry created over a period of three decades.

give Andy the business regardless of its value.

•   Have your estate representative exchange the voting stock for one-half voting shares for Andy and one-half non-voting shares for Becky. Her stock pays an 8 percent dividend, and she has an option to sell it to Andy on workable terms. If the corporation misses a dividend, her shares become voting, ahead of his.

•   Andy acquires a $2 million life insurance policy on your life now and agrees to purchase shares with the proceeds. Or, he gets a discount for his business efforts and you allow him to acquire shares from the estate at, say, 25 percent off. The business uses a split dollar plan to help him with premiums, and the insurance proceeds belong to Becky.

CAUTION: When there is a family buy-sell agreement, value under the law holds strictly to what a willing buyer will pay a willing seller. Therefore, if the business is really worth $2 million, be prepared to include this amount in your estate tax base, notwithstanding any discount Andy receives. The IRS has also argued that where children don't exercise a discount option, they make a gift to the estate. In fact, "bargain" family buy-sell arrangements have even caused the loss of a marital deduction. The bottom line is that family buy-sell agreements are a risky proposition, and invite dealings with the IRS.[13] That's why combining bequests and

---

13 James E. Roper, "Estee Lauder Loses Round in IRS Battle," Newhouse News Service, *The Star Ledger,* Jan. 4, 1993, p. 2. Joseph H. Lauder was cofounder of EJL Corp. with his wife, Estee Lauder. When Joseph died, a buy-sell agreement gave his family the right to acquire his shares. At issue was whether the agreement was an invalid device to pass stock to heirs at an artificially low price. The IRS gave the

life insurance is usually a better solution.

My recommendation: This is not about whether one child is more "deserving" than another. What's important after you are gone is their relationship with each other. Therefore, it's better to "err" (if you must) on the side of equality instead of fairness when it comes to bequeathing assets to children.

ERROR # 4:

Not Having A Flexible "Sell" Strategy While You Are Alive. It's not always possible to divide a family business among several children, or equalize with non-business assets for inactive children. If the truth actually be known, your children might opt to sell the business at the first chance or take it "public," anyway. After all, there is a tendency nowadays to try one's own skills and break away from the traditional family store or farm. The only solution may be a "top dollar" sale while you are alive.[14]

The time to sell, of course, is when everything is proceeding smoothly, and this may be when you are in your 60s, or even your 50s. Don't overlook the following strategies when-

estate an extra tax bill of $12 million. But this isn't the Lauder's only tax problem. In an attempt to avoid "millions" of capital gains taxes, Estee and her son, Ronald, apparently entered into some well-publicized stock maneuvers with other family members. Then the Clinton administration proposed legislation to ensnare them (and others who do the same.) These laws became part of the Taxpayer "Relief" Act of 1997. See Floyd Norris, "New Tax Law Takes Aim at Estee Lauder," *The New York Times*, Aug. 12, 1997, p.9.

14 Of course, the sale needn't be made to someone outside the business. In *Business Continuation Briefs*, a publication of PT Marketing, the author describes "The Buyer Down The Hall-How Key Employees Can Be The Key To Successful Ownership Transition."

SOMEDAY SON, THIS WILL ALL BE HERS.

ever a sale looms as the best solution:

· To avoid capital gains taxes, transfer the business to a charitable remainder trust (CRT) first, and name an independent trustee. Then the trust can sell shares, or your corporation can redeem them. You might even establish an Employee Stock Ownership Plan (ESOP) that acquires your shares from this trust.

· To reduce estate and gift taxes, especially when the business is an S Corporation, transfer your shares to a Grantor Retained Annuity Trust (GRAT) when the value is low. This trust makes payments to you for a period of time and then to your spouse for life. When values have increased and there is a sale or public acquisition, your children's GRAT receives future growth between now and then, and that growth is, of course, part of the sale.

· To sell a business to family, use an installment sale. This "freezes" the value at today's price, so all future upside belongs to your children. If you add an appropriate mortality risk premium to the sale price, this is a self-canceling installment note (SCIN). With a SCIN, installments cease at your death, and any remaining payments that would otherwise be due aren't included within your estate tax base.

· To sell a business to family when you're in relatively poor health, use a private annuity: Here, a family member makes payments that cease automatically at your death. Private annuities don't have a SCIN mortality risk premium, and they are useful when your expected life span is at least 1½ years. Be aware that if your expectancy is one year or less, the IRS will likely treat the transaction as a gift of the full sale price.

CAUTION: CRTs, ESOPs, GRATs, GRITs and SCINs are acronyms for complex legal and financial structures. I've introduced a few of them to give you some idea of how they are used in family business planning. Each involves either a sale or gift, and the advice of an experienced tax lawyer is required before taking action.

COMMON FINANCIAL AND INSURANCE ERRORS

ERROR # 1:

Inadequate "Key-Person" Insurance. In a well-known Emeloid court case, Judge Staley said, "What corporate purpose could be considered more essential than key man insurance? The business that insures its buildings, machinery and automobiles from every possible hazard can hardly be expected to exercise less care in protecting itself against the loss of two of its most vital assets—managerial skill and experience." I couldn't put it any better.

Real life examples speak ever so loudly. Consider the Sikes Corporation and its founder, Jimmy Sikes, who died of a heart attack in August of 1982, at age 52.[15] Six years before Mr. Sikes died, the company insured him for $6.9 million dollars. Initially, it was difficult to pay the annual premium

---

15 "When the Man is the Company," *Forbes*, March 28, 1983.

of $200,000, when annual earnings were only $370,000. But as the chief financial officer put it, "It (the life insurance) was just another of the costs of doing business". Other top executives remarked, "It's most useful in cases like ours; companies that are highly leveraged or dominated by one person." As you would expect, after Jimmy's death, the company immediately insured its new chief executives, one of whom is Board Chairman, Leon Sikes (Jimmy's brother).

Sometimes, tragedy strikes and keeps on striking. During a three-month period in 1982-83, Texasgulf, Inc. lost its board chairmen and four other top officials in a plane crash, and Arrow Electronics also lost 13 top employees in an electrical fire.[16] You wonder if these executives were well-insured![17]

My recommendation: In business, there is always a need for cash. First things first. Insure the lives of key people. It's just one of the costs of doing business!

ERROR #2:

The Corporation Names An Individual As Beneficiary Of Insurance. Speaking of life insurance, it's not unusual for a business policy to name an individual as beneficiary.

16 "Firms Feel Tragic Loss of Execs," *Rocky Mountain News,* February 17, 1981, p. 10B.

17 Even charities need life insurance on founders and key contributors. Consider the tragic case of folksinger John Denver who flew his airplane into Monterey Bay on Oct. 13, 1997. In 1984, a friend of mine sold Windstar Foundation a $1 million life insurance policy on Denver's life. In 1988, it canceled this policy because the $2,805 annual premium was *too expensive.* Some suggest that now the Denver estate is in trouble. See Norm Clarke, "Norm! Talk of the Town," *Rocky Mountain News,* Dec. 9, 1997, p. 6A. Perhaps the insurance cash would have come in handy.

Unfortunately, the tax results can be disastrous.

Let's suppose a corporation insures the founding owner as part of a business loan arrangement. The company is owner-beneficiary, and this policy is assigned to a creditor "as its interest may appear." The idea is that the lender is secured, and any balance after payment belongs to the original beneficiary: the corporation. Eventually, the loan is repaid, and the corporation elects to name an insured's spouse as beneficiary.

The result: At death, the proceeds are surely taxable income to the recipient. The theory is that the corporation either made a distribution of earnings to a shareholder or a deferred payment of compensation to a stockholder's beneficiary. Although there is some inconsistent law on this matter, expect the worst: The IRS will tax the insurance cash, and there won't be any income tax deduction.

My recommendation: When a corporation owns a key-person life insurance policy, name the company beneficiary also. Then, if you wish, have a separate agreement that permits a corporate tax deduction for reasonable deferred compensation payments on behalf of the former employee.

ERROR # 3:

Defining Life Insurance As Part Of A Deferred Compensation Agreement. An "unfunded" deferred compensation agreement between a corporation and its key employee that defers payments of future salary or bonuses will probably have the following straightforward tax consequences:

Payments that are taxable to the executive (or a beneficiary) when received;

Payments that are tax deductible by the corporation when made; and

No legal requirements to include other employees under similar arrangements.

There is, however, one Federal court case that causes business tax advisors to shudder: the 1980 case of *Dependahl v. Falstaff Brewing Corp.* In *Dependahl,* the judge found that a deferred compensation death benefit backed by life insurance is a "funded," and not an "unfunded," plan.

The result: A funded plan can bankrupt a company. The reason is that, under the law, these programs require that an employer cover all eligible employees similarly.

My recommendation: Although the Dependahl decision is highly criticized, it's best that all deferred compensation plans:

Not be referred to as an insured plan;

Not mention life insurance that is informally purchased by the corporation to "backstop" payments; and

Not describe benefits that are "tied to" a specific insurance policy.

ERROR # 4:

Undocumented Deferred Compensation. Sometimes, a corporation has an "oral understanding" with the founder regarding compensation at retirement. Yet, there is no formal written plan to put teeth in the arrangement. This can cause problems with both the IRS and U.S. Labor Department. Here's an example that explains why:

Ed Jones, the president of Jones Corp. is approaching age 65. Ed works only occasionally, but Jones Corp. pays him $5,000 per month indefinitely as a "token" salary for his many years of service.

Since Ed isn't currently performing services, the IRS will likely disregard the corporate tax deduction for Ed's payments. Secondly, a deferred compensation program must be in writing under the Employee *Retirement Income* Security Act of 1974 (ERISA).[18] Without a written document, there are potentially fines and criminal penalties under this law.

My recommendation: As far ahead as possible, all deferred (retirement) plans should be written and signed by the parties. In these agreements, explain the reasons why any future payments are proper when both past and current services are considered. (This also helps substantiate tax deductions for reasonable compensation.) Your lawyer may wish to file the plan with the Labor Department, too, depending on who is covered under the document.

ERROR # 5:

A (C) Corporation Stock Redemption Plan. The IRS is sensitive to transactions where a C corporation acquires the stock of a deceased stockholder. Unless all the shares are

---

18 Staff of the Securities and Exchange Commission have *informally* indicated that where employees voluntarily defer salary money into a pool of funds managed by the employer, these interests may also be securities. Perhaps a securities lawyer should review the arrangements. See remarks of Lawrence Brody, *Non Qualified Deferred Compensation*, Business Planning Video Teleconference Lecture Outline, the American College, American Society of CLU and ChFC, Dec. 3, 1997, pp. 105-107.

purchased, the entire sale price may be a taxable dividend, and this can be particularly devastating to a family corporation. Let me explain with this example:

The Smith Corporation is owned equally by Mom, Dad and Junior. Dad dies, and the company acquires his one-third interest. Under the law, however, his estate still owns Mom and Junior's shares because they are beneficiaries under his will. In other words, all family ownership is attributed to Dad, instead of merely the one-third portion he actually owned. *The result:* Not all of Dad's shares are acquired.

CAUTION: Fortunately, these complex "attribution" rules have exceptions that can somewhat soften tax consequences. But there are exceptions to the exceptions and exceptions to these exceptions. Be very careful that a C corporation acquires *all* outstanding shares (owned directly and indirectly) from the estate of a deceased shareholder. What's at stake are sale proceeds that are tax-free (or possibly fully taxed instead). Carefully following this area of tax law makes all the difference in the world.

ERROR # 6:

A Corporate Insured Buy-Sell Plan. It's popular to arrange a buy-sell stock redemption plan where the company insures each stockholder and agrees to purchase shares at death with the proceeds. It may seem easier to have a business pay the premiums, but this approach offers an inferior income tax result.

Imagine, for instance, a $2 million C corporation with two 50-50 stockholders (Joe and John). The business has a buy-sell agreement and insures each of them for $1 million. When Joe dies, the company acquires his shares income tax-free for $1 million. However, John doesn't receive a corresponding basis increase of $1 million on his shares. (If John acquires Joe's stock personally, John does, however, receive a basis increase.)

My recommendation: It's usually a better tax plan if stockholders agree to individually acquire each other's stock. In the above example, Joe acquires a $1 million policy insuring John, and John does the same for Joe. Their corporation pays most of the premiums under a split-dollar plan. Then, John can acquire Joe's shares at death and receive a $1 million basis in them.

Since it involves more policies, an individual stock purchase plan is more complicated than a corporate approach. For example, when there are three stockholders, each owns policies on the other two, *i.e.,* six policies instead of three. However, the tax advantages are well worth the complexities.

ERROR # 7:

Repositioning A (C) Corporation Insured Buy-Sell Plan Into An Individual Stock Purchase Plan. If there is presently a corporate buy-sell plan, it's possible to rearrange it into an individual stock purchase plan. However, there is a wrong and right way to do this.

The wrong way: As the wording in an agreement is modified, the company transfers policies to individual shareholders. For example, Joe receives John's policy, and John receives Joe's. When Joe dies, he is credited with a premium cost basis in the proceeds, but he pays income tax on the face amount less basis - a tax disaster!

The right way: Joe and John form a legitimate business partnership (perhaps to acquire a building for lease to their company). Then the corporation transfers insurance policies to their partnership. When Joe dies, the insurance cash is now tax-free. What a difference a little idea makes!

My recommendation: If you have an existing C corporation insured buy-sell plan, consider changing to an individual arrangement. However, be sure a new plan involves a partnership of stockholders, and not the individuals themselves.

ERROR # 8:

Liquidating Or Selling A Long-Time Family Corporation That Owns Profitable Real Estate. It was once popular (particularly in the mid-1900s) to convey land to corporations in a tax-free exchange for stock. In general, this gave a company the original owner's basis, which was probably quite low in comparison to the transferred value. Here's the problem: If the corporation is liquidated, and the land is distributed, there are now two taxes to pay. Consider this example:

Joe acquires land in 1950 for $10,000. He transfers it tax-free to his real estate corporation in 1960 for stock worth $20,000. Currently, this property is worth $250,000. If this company is liquidated, and the land is distributed to Joe, the corporation pays a capital gains tax on $240,000 ($250,000, less a $10,000 acquired basis). Then Joe also pays a tax on his stock profit. (If Joe dies and his company is liquidated, the corporation still pays a capital gains tax on $240,000, but fortunately, the estate's stock gets a basis step-up.)

My recommendation: Unfortunately, there really isn't an easy way for a capital asset rich C or S corporation to avoid capital gains taxes when it is liquidated, or when a corporation sells assets and distributes cash to stockholders. Perhaps the company can be sold instead to a purchaser who assumes the "inside" tax liability. Or before liquidating the corporation, appreciated property can be placed in a charitable remainder trust that sells it tax-free. Finally, if the corporation is maintained until Joe dies, the heirs at least receive a basis increase in his stock.

Family businesses are the backbone of our economy. Yet, most of these fragile entities are doomed to failure before they even begin. It appears that the solution is available if only two key factors are present: (1) The founder begins a succession plan the moment the business begins to succeed, and (2) the business owner searches for quality legal, insurance and financial advice. Help is available; it's simply one of the normal costs of doing business.

In the next chapter, we'll look at retirement planning, another planning issue where thinking ahead pays the best dividends.

CHAPTER 3

RETIREMENT INCOME:
SCARCITY OR SECURITY;
IT'S A STATE OF MIND

I f you're a regular reader of *USA Today*, you may have come across an article warning the oldest of the baby boomers, if not all the baby boomers, to consider how they'll maintain their present life-style when they stop working.[1] That's not bad advice. With potentially increased life expectancies, it's not too early to begin thinking about the money you'll need between the ages of 70 and 90.[2] This chapter will help you to think clearly about what you'll need and how to plan for your retirement.

---

1 Anne Willette and John Waggoner, "Strategies for a Secure Retirement," *USA Today*, March 7, 1997, p. 7D, and Dave Skidmore, "Retirement Optimism Up," Associated Press, *Rocky Mountain News*, Oct. 17, 1997. Mr. Skidmore quotes Jeffrey Love, Senior Research Associate for the AARP who cautions that most workers have a false confidence about financial freedom in retirement. Mr. Love is afraid that the money won't be there when they are.

2 For an *excellent* article on this subject, read Barbara O'Neill, "Planning After 60: Financial Concerns of Older Americans," *Journal of Financial Planning*, Aug. 1996, p. 68.

THE SEVEN DEADLY MISTAKES OF RETIREMENT PLANNING –

AND HOW TO AVOID THEM

MISTAKE #1:

A Passive Attitude About Retirement. One way to get yourself in trouble is to remain ignorant about the basics. When the late 7th District Congressman, Larry MacDonald, died, aides mentioned that his wife wasn't entitled to retirement income *because he hadn't signed up for the Congressional Pension Plan.*[3] This is a painful example, but it illustrates what can happen if we don't pay attention to our financial affairs.

Another common mistake is assuming it's too late to start a savings plan. Even if you have just retired, there's a strategy for you. You can begin a new "stay-at-home" business - a chance to have fun and become an entrepreneur for the first time. It's all a matter of how you look at it.

Relying too much on your employer can also trip you up. Unfortunately, most modern employers don't take a paternal role in providing for their employees' retirement. For instance, tax-qualified plans have largely shifted from *employer-guaranteed* defined benefit pensions to *employee-financed* 401(k) plans. The best strategy is to take advantage of what's available - sign up for the maximum early on and keep with it.

---

3 See "Tryggvi MacDonald Tries to Carry On," *The East Cobb Neighbor*, Nov. 10, 1983, p. 6B.

Don't overestimate, or depend too much, on Social Security and Medicare benefits. You already know it's foolish to depend on social programs for retirement income.[4] That is the hard reality of today's financial and political environment, so just consider all government benefits as "extra."

Don't forget to consider the effects of inflation. It seems that statistical inflation is slowing considerably during the '90s. Yet, the costs of sporting events, musicals and entertainment continue to rise. In the final analysis, it's a matter of supply and demand.

Another common mistake is relying too much on others for advice. Seniors depend on friends, family (and yes - even phone solicitors and high-pressure salespeople) for financial advice. The best approach is to (1) be proactive, (2) find a quality financial or retirement planner, (3) pay them for assistance, and (4) monitor the results yourself.

MISTAKE #2:

Withdrawing Money From 401(k) And Individual Retirement Accounts (IRAs) Without Tax Savvy. According to Sandra Phillips, an academic associate of The College of Financial Planning (a division of the National Endowment for Financial Education), 3 million taxpayers are penalized each year for mistakes when they take money out of their 401(k)s and IRAs.[5] For convenience, I'll refer to these as "QPs"- qualified plans.

---

4 As if it was unexpected, Alan Greenspan has officially warned Congress that the Social Security system is "badly underfunded." See William M. Walsh, "Greenspan says Social Security is in Trouble," *USA Today,* Nov. 21-23, 1997.

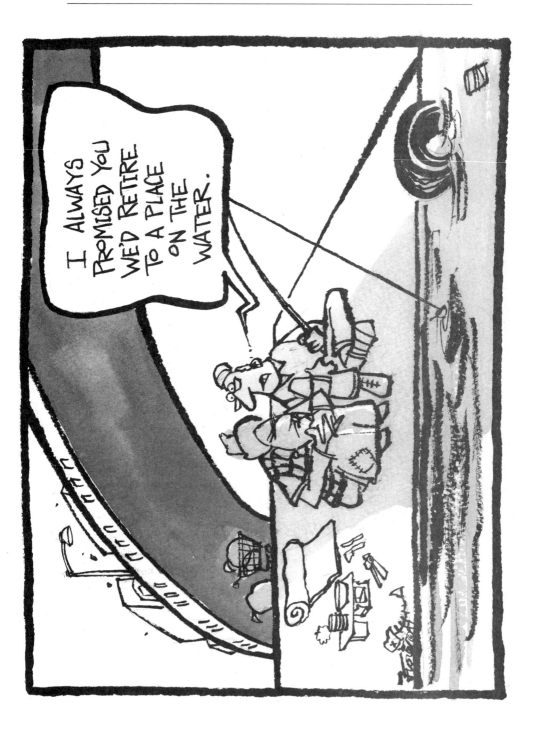

Here are the taxes or "tax traps" that you can expect on distributions from your QP:

· **Multiple States' Income (And Inheritance Taxes).** If you have made contributions as a resident of a high-tax state such as California, and now live in a low-tax state such as Florida, it's possible that you'll be "tracked down" by your former state government when you or your heirs receive taxable distributions. To avoid taxes in more than one state, you have a legal battle on your hands.

· **Federal Estate Taxes.** There weren't any in the past, but now they must be considered.

· **Income Taxes On Individual IRA Rollovers.** Let's say you terminate employment and take a distribution of $100,000 from a 401(k) plan. Your employer automatically withholds 20 percent ($20,000), and you receive $80,000. If you rollover this amount to an IRA within 60 days, you'll avoid income taxes, but you must have $100,000 (not just $80,000);[6] if not, you'll shelter only $80,000 from income tax, and you may owe a 10 percent early distribution penalty (excise tax) also on $20,000.

My recommendation: Have the 401(k) plan make a *direct* rollover of $100,000 to your IRA account, and there won't be any taxes withheld.

· **A 10 Percent Tax On Early Distributions.** Unless you are disabled (there are a few other exceptions), expect to

---

5 "Retirement Mistakes Can Become Extremely Costly," The Associated Press, *The News Tribune,* Tacoma, Wa., Oct. 7, 1996, Fifty Plus Section, p.5.

6 The $20,000 withheld by your employer is kept by the IRS and applied to your overall tax bill. They (not you) have the use of this money in the meantime.

pay a 10 percent excise tax if you withdraw funds prior to age 59½. (This tax actually raises a Federal income top tax rate from 39.6 percent to 49.6 percent.)

My recommendation: If you must withdraw from a QP account pre-59½, a financial advisor can give you reading material on strategies that avoid this tax.

· **A 50 Percent Penalty Tax If You Start Withdrawals Too Late.** You must begin taking at least minimum distributions by April 1st of the year after you reach 70½. If not, you'll pay a 50 percent excise tax on the amount you fail to take - the IRS wants its money *now*.

These taxes are certainly painful. They are examples of what can happen when Congress legislates the way "it ought to be." If you get expert advice on how to avoid these tax traps, however, I'm sure you'll conclude that tax deferral make this effort worthwhile.[7] I wish you the best.

MISTAKE #3:

Not Balancing Between Qualified Plan (QPs, 401(k)s And IRAs), And Non-Qualified (NQ) Personal Savings Strategies. There is so much emphasis on tax-deferral, you'd

---

7 Have you heard of the Roth IRA, a product of the Taxpayer Relief Act of 1997, a strategy sponsored by Sen. William Roth, a Delaware Republican? If your annual adjusted gross income is less than $95,000, ($150,000 if married) you may contribute up to $2,000 per year to a tax sheltered retirement account. Although the contribution isn't tax deductible, all withdrawals are tax-free, and there is no 10 percent withdrawal penalty pre-age 59½. To some, this strategy seems almost magical. Mary Rowland, "What Congress Has Roth," *Dow Jones Investment Advisor,* Nov., 1997, p. 151-152. For an analysis of whether to change an existing IRA to a Roth IRA, ask a financial advisor for a copy of "Should You Convert Your Current IRA to a Roth IRA in 1998?", *Journal of Financial Planning,* Dec., 1997, by Peter J. Melcher, J.D., LL.M., Lucy Arend, J.D. and James Howicz, J.D., p. 64.

think that QP accounts are the only way to accumulate for retirement. This simply isn't true. However, there are really five growth philosophies you can take when setting aside money for the future. Each involves the effect of income taxes - and some traps and pitfalls, too:

·   *QPs,* where you (or your employer) deduct what is saved, and you pay taxes (and sometimes penalty taxes) when you withdraw. You gain the use of tax savings and tax deferral, in the meantime.[8]

·   *Life insurance,* where you gain tax deferral and can borrow or withdraw values tax-free. The traps occur when you surrender the policy and pay tax on distributions that exceed premium cost basis.

·   *Annuities,* where you gain tax deferral but eventually pay tax on profit withdrawals at ordinary income rates. There may be penalty taxes, too, on payments before age 59½

·   *Growth stocks* and *real estate,* where you gain tax deferral (until sale) and eventually pay tax at lower capital gains rates.

·   *Mutual funds,* where you pay tax on distributions (mostly at capital gains rates) along the way. This increases basis, however, which lowers taxes on withdrawals at a later date.

---

8 You may also gain protection when someone throws a lawsuit your way. Consider the matter of O. J. Simpson. Read Abigail Goodman's article, "Law Shields O. J.'s Pension," Los Angeles Times, *The Denver Post,* June 13, 1997, where the author explains that Simpson could draw $25,000 per month from his profit sharing account without ever turning a penny of it over to satisfy the $33.5 million civil suit judgment against him.

CAUTION: QP accounts that legitimately avoid and defer taxes are nearly an unbeatable strategy. As I've outlined, however, there can be a heavy price to pay when you withdraw money too early or you don't take enough. *And, the laws can change at a moment's notice.*[9]

My recommendation: You should balance retirement savings between QPs and personal strategies. I recommend these additional steps to financial security and success:

1.   First, keep your "quick access" money in permanent level premium life insurance where you can easily obtain loans and withdrawals without paying taxes. The tax-deferred, penalty tax-free cash values also act as a resource in case of an emergency. (Also, consider muni-bond mutual funds, where you can obtain cash at a moment's notice.)

2.   For the long-term, use 401(k)s and IRAs for tax deductions and tax deferral. Although a 401(k) plan may permit tax-free loans (that must be repaid), these programs are really designed for when you are age 60 or later because of excise taxes on distributions pre-59½.

3.   Acquire personal growth mutual funds where there is an additional long-range investing goal. You pay some taxes currently, but mostly at reduced long-term capital gains rates.

4.   If you have extra funds, hold individual growth securities that don't pay dividends. Here, you gain long-range tax-deferred growth (until sale), and the profit will be long-

---

9 Prior to the Taxpayer Relief Act of 1997, there was a 10 percent excise tax when the law deemed too much was taken from a QP or IRA. With the 1997 legislation, Congress canceled this tax immediately.

term capital gains at lower rates.

5. Finally, purchase annuities (variable or fixed) where the profit is tax-deferred, and eventually taxed at ordinary income rates. Keep in mind that most withdrawals from annuities pre-59½ incur a 10 percent penalty tax; in a 39.6 percent bracket, this has the effect of increasing your rate to about *50* percent.

To summarize, you can have balance using these five savings strategies. You gain advantages from each method, and with careful timing, it's possible to avoid the traps and pitfalls associated with any one approach.

MISTAKE #4:

Not Acquiring Life Insurance In A 401(k) Plan. In a qualified pension or 401(k) plan it's possible to purchase insurance on the life of a participant. The proceeds become part of his or her benefits under the plan, and are ultimately paid to a personal beneficiary. There is an additional *advantage*: The face amount of the policy (less cash values at death) is free from Federal income tax and most state income tax as well.

A 401(k) plan can permit you to use up to 100 percent of your account for cash value whole life coverage (25 percent for term insurance). The insured(s) can be you, your spouse, your children, parents, a business partner, or some combination of these. This benefit can really "super-charge" a retirement account. Here are a few situations where you might acquire life insurance in a 401(k) plan:

Example #1: A 401(k) account is owner-beneficiary of a $250,000 policy insuring your mother. At her death, the cash value is $50,000. Since the "at risk" amount is $200,000, this can be distributed to you now without paying income or excise taxes. You use this money for estate taxes and debts in your mother's estate.

Example #2: You name your spouse, Mary, beneficiary of a 401(k) account. But the account insures you for $150,000 and with her agreement, this will be payable to your children from a previous marriage. At your death, this account pays $150,000 to the children, and Mary takes an income from the remainder of your retirement fund.

Example #3: You have a separate agreement to acquire your co-owner's stock for $500,000. A 401(k) account insures your co-owner's life for this amount. At death, this account distributes "at risk" insurance proceeds to you for the stock purchase, and there are no income or excise taxes on this money. In order to always have $500,000 tax-free in the policy, your account acquires a "type B" policy that pays a face amount in addition to its cash values.

Example #4: You have a large $2 million account in a 401(k) plan. When income and estate taxes are considered, the account is worth only $400,000 for your family. So, you acquire a $2 million policy in the 401(k) plan. In a few years, the policy is distributed, and you pay income taxes on the cash values - when they are relatively low. Your advisors make arrangements to protect the policy from any new income, excise or estate taxes. The *result:* Your family is assured of $2 million instead of a mere $400,000 net. In addition, they have the balance of your 401(k) account.

CAUTION: Life insurance in a 401(k) account provides a remarkable planning opportunity. Be aware, however, that (1) the plan must specifically permit you to direct the use of your account for insurance premiums, and (2) the IRS requires plan administrators to report to you a small taxable amount each year (the so-called PS58 or pure cost of insurance based on the life of the person your account insures), whenever funds are used for premiums. This counts as a basis, however, (on the policy's taxable cash value portion of a death benefit), when proceeds of the policy are actually distributed.

MISTAKE #5:

No Specific Distribution Strategy At Age 70 1/2. It seems that everyone is on the IRA and 401(k) bandwagon nowadays. Since most contributions are made early in the year, this money is sometimes referred to as "fuel" for the stock market especially between January and April 15th. And Congress is always considering making these QPs more appealing to individuals.[10] (Could this solve those Social Security funding issues that seem to keep us on our toes?)

As tax-deferred QP accounts increase in value, it's possible to imagine a *major* planning issue down the road - the need for a philosophy on how to withdraw payments from an IRA or 401(k) plan. In my opinion, this is the number

---

10 See note 9, *supra.*

one financial planning problem as well as an *opportunity* that's ahead for the successful QP investor.

Let's say that it's 1997 and you are age 55 or 56. You have accumulated $500,000 in a QP account and expect to earn 10 percent on average until you begin receiving distributions. *The good news:* With no additional contributions, you'll have at least $2 million on hand by age 70. *The bad news:* Without a well-arranged distribution plan at age 70½ when you must begin taking payments, you may lose most of this account to taxes. Since the rules are extremely complex, I'm including some pointers that should be quite helpful:

1.   By April 1ˢᵗ following the calendar year when you reach age 70½, you must take your first payment – or pay an extra 50 percent excise tax, in addition to income taxes, on what isn't taken. *You must receive a second payment by the end of this same calendar year.*

2.   Unless you elect that your account purchase an annuity policy, you must make an irrevocable[11] decision to *recalculate* or *not recalculate* the payout based on a projected life span. Once this decision is made, it cannot be changed. *The good news:* your payout method merely establishes the *minimum* amount to withdraw - you can always take more!

Recalculation offers the possibility of a slower and longer payout period and greater income tax-deferral, as long as you continue to live. For instance, at actual age 70, the life

11 In one situation, before age 70½. an individual named a spouse beneficiary. At age 70½ , the beneficiary was changed to the estate. Unfortunately, the IRS didn't permit an amended change back to the spouse.

expectancy is 16 years. If you *don't* recalculate, your QP annual payment is determined with divisors of 1/16, 1/15, 1/14, 1/13, 1/12, etc., and after 16 years it will all be distributed. If you redetermine your life expectancy each year, the divisors are 16, 15.3, 14.6, 13.9, 13.2, etc.. (You'll even be receiving benefits at age 90 - when the divisor is 5 - and beyond.) With recalculation, the divisor is larger, the payment is less, distributions are spread over a longer period, and the account earns tax-deferred interest longer. The problem is that when you die, your recipient must cash-out and pay taxes in the year after your death – all at once.

Example #1: At age 70½, you have a $2 million IRA and a recalculation distribution plan; your estate is the beneficiary. The first year's payment is $125,000 ($2 million ÷ 16.) Your account is worth $2,100,000 when you take the second distribution of $137,255 ($2.1 million ÷ 15.3.) If you don't recalculate, the second year's distribution is $140,000 ($2.1 million ÷ 15.)

The tax disaster: Let's say you recalculate, and die after the second year when there is an account balance of $2.2 million. Your heirs pay income taxes, if any, on this account during the calendar year after the year of death.[12] If your distribution method is non-recalculation, the account balance is payable over the next 14 (16 minus 2) years - that's quite a different tax planning result!

Example #2: In 1997 at age 70½, you have a $2 million

---

12 If you die before 70½ (with no named beneficiary), your estate beneficiary has five years to cash-out your account.

IRA account. Your wife, Mary, is age 68, and your daughter, Judy, is 43. Since you're married, it's possible to combine Mary's life expectancy with yours when determining a payout divisor. You can (a) recalculate both life expectancies; (b) recalculate your life span - no recalculation for Mary; (c) recalculate her life span - no recalculation for you; or (d) recalculate neither life expectancy.

For instance, by using two recalculations– (a) above - the divisors are 21.5, 20.7, 19.8, 19.0, 18.2, etc. By recalculating you alone - (b) above - the divisors are 21.5, 20.2, 19.4, 18.5, and 17.3, and by recalculating neither - (d) above - the divisors are 21.5, 20.5, 19.5, 18.5 and 17.5. Obviously, when both life spans are recalculated, and the divisors are larger, the payout plan is slowest and longest.

My recommendation: Recalculate only *your* life expectancy. If you die first, Mary has a special privilege under the tax law. She can rollover what's left of your IRA to a new spousal IRA. She takes distributions over her life expectancy (or if she is not age 70½, she can wait until then). If her death occurs *before* yours, continue using your remaining life expectancy at the time. Thereafter, if you die before age 88, your daughter, Judy, can stretch-out payments until 2015, because her mother, Mary, had a 17.6 life expectancy when you were age 70½ and she was 68 (and 17.6 plus 70.5 equals slightly more than 88).

If you die first and Mary elects a rollover to her IRA, she then names Judy as beneficiary and claims her as a measuring life. The law requires that Judy use an artificial age *10 years younger* than Mary: Therefore, if at your death, Mary is age 71, she must use age 61 for measuring Judy's life span (and then 72/62, 73/63, 74/64, etc.). Mary can recalculate, but Judy cannot.

Finally, let's say that Mary dies when Judy is actually age 55. Judy can "stretch out" payments over her true remaining IRS life expectancy which then is 28.6 years. During the next five years, she'll use divisors of 28.6, 27.6, 26.6, 25.6, 24.6, etc., in determining her annual payments.[13]

Let's say you've spent many years protecting a tax-deferred QP account. By having a carefully arranged distribution plan, you'll maximize continuation of this tax shelter and leverage its value into multigenerational wealth for you, your spouse, children and grandchildren. Without a plan, the whole thing will someday come crashing down in a heap. This needn't happen!

I know that the above rules are extremely complex, but please become familiar with this law. It's your money, and you just can't afford to make an error.[14]

My recommendation: (1) Be a proactive student of pension distributions law; (2) work closely with a financial coun-

13 It's important that Judy not miss the next IRA payment after Mary's death. Recently, there was a tax disaster in a similar situation according to a *Forbes* magazine article: Laura Saunders, "The Six Commandments," *Forbes,* June 17, 1996. Apparently, a 31-year old Tennessee man missed an IRA beneficiary payment deadline after his mother died pre 70½. (This payment was due by Dec. 31st of the year following the calendar year of her death.) The result: This IRA tax shelter expired in five years, instead of gradually over the next 51! This story just illustrates the significance of good (and bad) planning. This gentleman and his advisor should have known better!

selor; and (3) have a tax lawyer occasionally verify that pension law is the same. You just never know when it will change.

MISTAKE #6:

No QP Tax Liquidity Strategy. If your distribution strategy is to leverage a valuable QP account into multigenerational values, then it is essential to have a tax liquidity plan on the side.

Let's refer once more to the above example where your wife, Mary, elects a rollover strategy for the QP account that remains at your death. By doing this, she defers paying any income taxes that are otherwise due in a lump.

CAUTION: When Mary dies and transfers this rollover IRA (and any QP accounts that she owns, too) to her daughter, Judy, Judy then pays estate and excise taxes on the value of these assets. If you and Mary don't have a tax liquidity plan outside the QP accounts, it will probably be necessary for Mary's personal representative to liquidate them. When this happens, *income taxes are due all at once.* It's likely total taxes will be 75-80 percent, and Judy will lose a tax-deferred "shelter" which might have paid her a lifetime income.

My recommendation: Maintain a tax liquidity fund *outside* your QP accounts. A good example is a last survivor insurance policy that insures you and your spouse. And, if you are at least 59½, you might withdraw from the IRA

---

14 Unfortunately, even the "experts" trip up and make errors when it comes to pension money. See David Cay Johnston, "For Some, Pensions Still Find Ways to Disappear," *The New York Times,* May 18, 1997. As this article infers, it always pays dividends to pay attention to your own pension fund.

enough money to pay the premiums.

In most cases, it's wise to leverage a large QP account by arranging a multigenerational program, as I have suggested. The tax-deferral potential is quite exciting. I strongly recommend that you establish an "outside" liquidity plan as well —life insurance guarantees the tax money and the successful leveraging of the plan.

MISTAKE #7:

No QP Designated Beneficiary Strategy. Just to see if you are paying "attention," let me repeat the most important example in this chapter.

In Mistake #5, Example #2, I described a situation where it is 1997 and you are age 70½; your wife, Mary, is 68, and she is listed as a designated beneficiary on your QP account. Your daughter, Judy, is contingent beneficiary. Your life span is recalculated annually, but Mary's is not. Therefore, if Mary dies first, you continue receiving payments using life spans established at your age 70½. At your death prior to age 88 (2015), Judy uses Mary's age 68 life span and spreads payments over the balance of a 17.6 year period. If you die first, Mary elects to rollover the balance of the QP account to her personal IRA, and defers income tax until she receives payments from her IRA. She combines Judy's life span with hers on the basis that Judy is 10 years younger. When Mary dies, Judy (at age 55) stretches remaining payments (no recalculation) on the basis of her 28.6-year fixed term actual life expectancy at the time. She pays any estate taxes with life insurance proceeds held "outside" Mary's estate tax base. Any questions?

This spouse-to-spouse-to-child(ren) beneficiary designation approach leverages the QP account on a multigenerational basis and achieves an excellent tax planning result for everyone concerned. There are, however, other beneficiary approaches that may be useful in certain situations depending on your circumstances:

Example #1: You are worried about the ability of Mary (or Judy) to manage money.

Example #2: Mary is your second or third spouse. Judy is your child from a previous marriage. You are concerned that Mary may leave your QP account to a new husband or someone besides Judy.

Example #3: When Mary elects a rollover IRA, it's not protected from judgment creditors under your state's law, and this alarms you.

Example #4: You don't have enough other assets to fund a $600,000 "exemption" trust (without specifying this trust as beneficiary of your QP account).

In each of these situations, you may prefer that a trust (or possibly Judy) be the designated beneficiary of your QP account. Be aware, however, that there are tax disadvantages if Mary is not the direct beneficiary (or possibly a beneficiary through an estate that acts as a conduit for her). For instance, at your death:

1. Only Mary can rollover your account to a new IRA and defer payments if she is not age 70½, and

2. If payments are coming directly from your 401(k) plan to Judy (or a trust for Mary or Judy), Mary must consent to your beneficiary designation; otherwise, she can dispute this if she has been married to you for one year. (On the other hand, she cannot make a challenge if the trust's payments are coming directly from an *IRA*.)

Presuming you still feel that Mary shouldn't be the direct payee, here are a few choices for "designated beneficiary" of your QP account:

· **Your Estate** - Unless this is merely a conduit for Mary, I don't recommend this approach, because an estate beneficiary is the same as *no* beneficiary. In one situation, however, the IRS actually permitted a spouse to rollover to her IRA when she was sole heir to an estate. Therefore, expect the law to require distribution in the calendar year that contains the fifth anniversary of your death.

· **Your Child, Children, Or Grandchildren** - If you prefer, you can establish separate IRA's for each. Be aware that there may be a 55 percent generation-skipping transfer tax whenever your QP funds are paid to a grandchild.

· **A Bypass $600,000 "Exemption" Trust** - If you are 70½, this trust must be irrevocable and legally effective or it cannot qualify as a "designated beneficiary" under the tax law. It then uses the life expectancy of its oldest beneficiary in calculating distributions. This produces a smaller divisor and focuses on a larger payment than when a younger person's life span is used.

· **A QTIP Trust** – This trust for Mary passes its assets

to your specified beneficiary when she dies. Keep in mind that the law doesn't permit Mary to rollover these trust funds to her personal IRA (unless perhaps she has a right to withdraw everything from the trust). Remember that whenever QP benefits are payable to trusts, the rules are extremely complicated and it's crucial to seek competent pension and estate tax planning help.[15]

· **A Charity** – Although legally a charity cannot be a designated beneficiary for purposes of calculating annual distributions, you can eliminate all income and estate taxes on a QP account after your death, by paying it to a charity after your death. If you are philanthropic, consider this possibility. Then you might take out a life insurance policy to "replace" these funds for your children or grandchildren. Remember, that whenever QP benefits are payable to trusts, the rules are extremely complicated and it's crucial to seek competent pension and estate-planning help.

Again, the "simplest" solution to beneficiary issues (and post age 70½ distributions) is to designate a spouse beneficiary, who plans to rollover to his or her IRA and designate children as new beneficiaries. If you feel this is "risky" because these children are from a previous marriage, then consider insuring your life for their benefit, and simply designate your spouse as the beneficiary of your QP account.

15 "See Taxes Due At Once on Revocable Trust," a New York Times feature published in the *Sun Sentinel,* Ft. Lauderdale, Nov. 1, 1993, Business section, p. 34. Quoting Seymour Goldberg, Esq., this article explains how a large IRA account was payable to a living trust that didn't qualify as a designated beneficiary. This was a tax disaster; the entire account was taxed to the trust in one year!

In Chapter 4, we'll talk about how to get the most from gift-giving strategies. Used properly, they can provide much personal satisfaction *and* save a significant amount in estate taxes. But you have to understand the subtleties. You can lose out on the benefits if you don't attend to the details properly.

CHAPTER 4

GIFTING TO LOVED ONES:

HOW TO MAKE GOOD IDEAS EVEN BETTER

Gift-giving can bring a lot of joy, but the promised benefits often lose out to confusion. You'd love to believe the consultant who says to you, "You just can't afford *not* to make $10,000 tax-free gifts under the law."[1] But doubts remain. You wonder: *Can I afford to do that? What happens if I need the money someday? Will my children save the money or spend it? Should I put some "strings" on the gift?*

Eventually, you may become comfortable with the idea of gifting. But you should be aware that there are numerous traps and pitfalls that can occur whenever you make the

---

1 Know that the $10,000 sum is indexed for inflation beginning Jan. 1, 1999. Also, INSGIFT, a software product of Insmark of San Ramon California, objectively determines whether one's assets will support the retirement income they need, given certain assumptions for inflation, rate of return and life expectancy. This financial planning aide also shows which assets (an IRA, cash, or an investment fund) are best to provide personal income. If you'd like more information, call me.

actual transfers. In the pages ahead, I'll acquaint you with
how gift-giving can "backfire" under the tax law. Don't fear:
I'll also ease your concerns. There are real solutions to these
problems, and I'll outline them for you in detail. Whenever
there is an issue associated with gifting, the law always provides an answer.

WHY GIFTING SAVES TAXES

Once upon a time, in the '60s and '70s, there were separate rates for Federal gift taxes and estate taxes. If you had $2
million and gifted $1 million, there was $1 million left in
the estate tax base. Gift and estate taxes were calculated sepa-
rately, and the tax on gifts was always less.

Today, the law begins by permitting a donor to make as
many tax-free gifts each year to as many people as he or she
wishes. (You can even add strangers to the list.) The only
limitation is that you can't give one person property worth
more than $10,000 annually, or the "excess" gift becomes
taxable.

Now, there is a unified gift and estate tax law that makes
taxable gifts (above $10,000) more complicated than in the
'60s and '70s The effect is that taxable lifetime gifts are added
to the estate tax base at death. An estate representative then
subtracts from the estate tax, the gift tax, if any, that was
paid earlier when the transfer was made. Keep in mind that
with the current law, each taxable gift potentially moves you
and the estate into higher transfer tax brackets. It's as if this
year's earnings are added to next year's (and the next) to de-

termine the income tax rate you'll pay. Here's how this "uni-fied" system actually works.

The first $600,000 gifted (not counting $10,000 gifts) is gift tax-free, but this doesn't make it exempt from estate taxes. Let's say you have $2 million and gift $600,000 now. At death, the estate tax base is still $2 million ($1.4 million actually) in the estate, plus the previous gift of $600,000). The transfer tax is calculated on $2 million, even though the estate "owns" merely $1.4 million. The estate tax is $588,000, and this is precisely the tax your personal repre-sentative would pay if you hadn't made the earlier gift.

The good news: If a $600,000 gift is worth $800,000 when you die, the $200,000 profit at that time isn't part of the estate tax base.

There is yet another reason to make a large lifetime gift. Here is a riches-to-poverty example that makes its point:

You have a $2.588 million estate, and gift two children $1 million each. There is just enough left ($588,000) to pay the gift tax on these transfers. You die three years later - broke. An estate representative includes this $2 million gift in the estate tax base and calculates a tax of $588,000. But since you paid a gift tax of $588,000 earlier, this is subtracted. And the net estate tax is zero. On the other hand, let's say you don't make the $2 million gift. Now, there is a $2.588 million estate tax base (instead of $2 million) at death. How-ever, the tax isn't $588,000 (on $2 million) – the tax is $857,180 (on $2.588 million).

Why this difference? Well, since you lived three years past

the gift, the IRS tells your representative to exclude $588,000 of gift tax from the estate tax base. *The result:* Your estate "saves" the estate tax on the gift tax that you paid earlier. Voila! A complex tax break perhaps, but this aspect of the transfer tax law has become popular with successful taxpayers who feel comfortable making lifetime transfers to family members.

With this last bit of good news, here is the bad news – the traps and pitfalls just waiting for the unwary.

GIFTING: MISTAKES TO AVOID

MISTAKE #1:

Not Starting Early Enough. If you are comfortable in your 30s and 40s sharing possessions with family (instead of starting gift programs in your 50s and 60s), the mathematics of gift tax planning can be compelling.[2] Don't forget the all-important, $10,000 per donee annual exclusion.

Let's say you have three married children. It's possible to gift them $60,000 annually ($1.2 million over a 20-year period). If a spouse makes gifts, too (or consents to your doing this), annual tax-free gifts can be increased to $20,000 for each donee, or $2.4 million overall.

Moreover, with a little planning there are some extra advantages to establishing an early gift-giving plan. Advisors will probably suggest gifting nonvoting shares in a family

2 In *Made In America, My Story,* Doubleday, 1992, Sam Walton proudly refers to a family limited partnership he formed in 1953 to which he gave some sizable holdings. He advocates giving property away early on before it appreciates. This is the best way to avoid owing estate taxes eventually.

limited partnership (FLP) or business. You'll probably be entitled to "discount" these gifts by 30 percent or more because shares that can't vote aren't worth very much in the open market.

Imagine a strategy where you own assets worth $1 million (that have a gift tax value of say $600,000) that may appreciate in 30-40 years to $8-10 million, or even more. By forming a family entity, you can gradually gift tax-free all but a small share of this enterprise, but yours is the only portion that votes. What's more, you maintain control and take a salary, as well. By making these gifts over a long period of time, nearly all the future value to children is shifted without paying a transfer tax, and you keep the management power. You'll also get to watch them enjoy the property along the way. Everyone benefits from the kind of gifting plan that is based on solid tax planning fundamentals and a willingness to share.[3]

CAUTION: No matter how attractive any gift-giving arrangement, if you don't feel comfortable parting with the property, don't do it (or at least make sure the plan is flexible and can be adjusted year by year). The tax savings aren't

---

3 There may be even more leverage by using a Grantor Retained Annuity Trust (GRAT). Here, you transfer shares in a family interest to a trust that makes a payment to you for a specific period of, say, 15 years. After the value of this income is subtracted from the gift, the *net gift may be practically zero.* Once you live the 15 years, the property belongs (nearly gift-free) to the children. You've shifted a significant asset and its appreciation to them without paying much in transfer taxes. A word of caution: If you die during the GRAT period (15 years in this example), your estate owes taxes on the value of trust assets at that time. Consider a life insurance policy that covers this obligation.

worth very much if there is uneasiness when you part with the asset.

MISTAKE #2:

Making Incomplete Gifts. I'm sure you've heard about the donor who gave away the farm; but forgot to record the deed. Or, perhaps an insured "gave" an insurance policy to a daughter, but made her the beneficiary of the policy, not the owner.

Who's kidding whom? To remove an asset from an estate, the owner always makes a complete transfer under state law. For instance, a gift check must be mailed by December 31st to make it this year's gift. The deed must also be recorded in a timely manner, and the insurance company should make changes on its books in the same year you transfer ownership of the policy.

CAUTION: To give it away, just make sure it's "gone." To be sure, ask an advisor what it takes to make a complete gift, even though the answer may seem obvious at the moment.

MISTAKE #3:

Making Taxable Gifts Indirectly. There are several situations where you may not intend to give, but the law imposes transfer taxes anyway. Each of the following possibilities has "gift tax logic," even though it may not initially be apparent:

Trap #1: *A Corporation "Sells" Land Worth $500,000 To Your Son (Bill) For $400,000. The result:* As owner of this

business, you probably make a gift to Bill of $100,000 because this is the amount of his bargain. The IRS may even say that you received a "constructive" dividend, and assess income taxes to you on $100,000. Why is this? Well, if there is a gift, you had to get the money somehow. Unfortunately, this is the kind of logic that makes most of us wonder why we've created such a complicated tax system.

Trap #2: *A Corporation Insures Your Life For $1 Million, And It Names Bill Beneficiary.* If your spouse, Mary, owns most of the stock when you die, she will probably make a $1 million "gift" to Bill when he receives the insurance money. Keep in mind that as owner of the business, she has a right at any time to change the beneficiary from Bill to the company. By choosing an individual, the money indirectly leaves the business under her direction. This result is similar to Trap #1 above.

Trap #3: *Being Named Guarantor Of A Child's Loan.* Your daughter, Judy, doesn't have a credit payment history. To assist her in obtaining a $500,000 mortgage, you sign on her loan papers as guarantor. Since she obtains money that probably wasn't available without help, there is a likely gift! The value of this transfer may be the difference between her interest rate and an alternative "usurious" rate available elsewhere. What's worse: If Judy defaults and her lender forecloses, there is a taxable gift of any amount you pay on her behalf.

Trap #4: *Interest-Free Loans To Children.* You loan a child $200,000 to start a business. The interest rate is 10 percent, but you excuse his payment of $20,000. This "foregone" interest is a gift, and if you forgive payments of principal, these are gifts also.

My recommendation: If there is the slightest doubt about making an indirect gift, consult tax advisors. Otherwise, someone may pay a tax when it's least expected.

MISTAKE #4:

Gifting Assets with Basis Higher Than True Value. Sometimes, people gift property that shows a loss. If it is sold later, a donee cannot show a tax deduction. For example, your basis is $150,000 in property worth $120,000. If you gift these assets to your son, there is no income tax deduction for the loss. But when he sells them for $140,000, he'll owe capital gains tax on his $20,000 "profit." If, instead, you first sell this property for $120,000 and gift the cash, there is a $30,000 loss which possibly can be deducted against other capital gains that you may incur.

My recommendation: Carefully examine the basis in each asset you intend to give; then sell "tax loss" assets, and gift the cash instead.

MISTAKE #5:

Gifting Low Basis Assets Instead of Cash. Most donors want to give illiquid assets that don't provide current cash flow. On the other hand, donees usually want cash or property that pays a current income.

Each point of view is understandable. But from a tax perspective, donors should give tax-paid cash, plain and simple.

Here's the reason. If you give stock worth $10,000 that costs zero or thereabouts, there is a capital gains tax liability of perhaps $2,000 "inside the gift," and there is no discount for this hidden income tax obligation.

My recommendation: It's better financially to gift $10,000 cash worth the full $10,000 than to gift $10,000 of stock that is worth $8,000 after taxes. Each gift uses a $10,000 annual exclusion, but the cash gift is simply more tax efficient because it transfers real value of $10,000.

MISTAKE #6:

Gifting Too Much. Those conscious about transfer taxes sometimes take their gift giving too seriously. For instance, I remember a "money" radio talk show where a Mr. Smith in his 60's owned assets worth about $1.6 million. Because of concern for paying estate taxes of about $450,000, his plan was to gift five children $1 million, at the rate of $50,000 each year for about 20 years. *The result:* His estate is reduced to $600,000, and there is no estate tax. But, there still may be a better way.

My recommendation: For perhaps only $15,000 annually, Mr. Smith can insure his life for approximately $450,000. (If children own his policy, they can use insurance cash to pay the estate tax.) This approach allows Mr. Smith to keep more of his assets, and it assures that his entire $1.6 million estate passes intact to his family at his death. Often, an insurance program allows everyone to spend more assets on themselves or others less fortunate. *Get the figures before gifting too much, too fast.*

MISTAKE #7:

Not Keeping Good Gifting Records. I know of several families who gift each heir $10,000 annually. Gifts are made at the same time each year directly to children and grandchildren, or indirectly to a trust for payment of premiums on a life insurance policy.

CAUTION: These families probably make other gifts as well, for birthdays, holidays, casual spending, cash for tuition, use of a car, etc., etc. Total gifts probably exceed $15,000-$20,000 per child, and no one seems concerned that these extra amounts are considered taxable gifts as well.

My recommendation: To my knowledge, the IRS does not usually attempt to collect tax on "incidental" transfers to family and friends. However, this is always a possibility. Simply put, take full advantage of the tax system, but legally. Then, keep good records just in case the IRS wants proof that gifting was within the $10,000 limits.

MISTAKE #8:

Making Bogus Gifts. Sometimes, gift-giving becomes the main focus of a wealth preservation plan. The objective is to determine as many donees as possible when it comes to $10,000 gifts.

For instance, suppose you are not expected to live more than 12 months. If gifts are made now and next January 1st (for a year or so), it may be possible to make a significant reduction in the eventual estate tax bill. It's possible to gift assets to children, grandchildren, nieces, nephews, and even in-laws and friends. But, let's say you make a $10,000 gift to a friend who agrees to turn over this money later to your son. This is a "bogus" gift that is also tax fraud.

CAUTION: Do not make transfers conditioned on a donee returning the gift; the penalties can be severe - even jail time.

MISTAKE #9:

Not Gifting Tuition And Medical Expenses. Those interested in making tax-free gifts sometimes forget that transfers to pay tuition and medical expenses aren't considered gifts (or generation-skipping transfers) under the tax law. Therefore, when everything is "on the table," it may be possible to gift someone much more than $10,000 annually.

For example, you give Bill $10,000 cash and also provide $16,000 for his tuition and health insurance premiums. Be sure to pay the tuition directly to an educational organization, and the medical expense must be paid to the party providing the insurance or service. *The result:* Bill receives (or benefits from) $26,000 without anyone paying a transfer tax.

CAUTION: Don't forget that the tuition and medical advances are not gift tax exempt if you give Bill the money to make the payments.

My recommendation: Have all tuition and medical expenses sent to you directly. Then, pay the institutions and keep copies of the checks.

If a wealthy relative or friend who is ill has a taxable estate and is interested in tax planning, suggest to him or her (in addition to making $10,000 gifts) that all children and grandchildren (and perhaps other relatives as well) submit outstanding tuition and medical expenses for payment. If one family line may benefit more than another, it's possible to "equalize" overall transfers later by adjusting inheritances when they are being distributed.

MISTAKE #10:

Not Splitting Gifts, If Married. A married person can gift someone up to $20,000 a year if his or her spouse consents to the gift. This enables a spouse who has most of the property to take advantage of another spouse's annual exclusion (and $600,000 "exemption" also). Consider these situations involving Harry, who is quite ill, and his wife, Mary:

Example #1: Harry's estate is worth exactly $600,000; Mary has $1 million. If each of them make $10,000 gifts, Harry's transfers don't reduce their taxes since his estate is already at, or less than, the $600,000 "exemption." Consequently, with Harry's consent, Mary should make a $10,000 gift for each of them. *The result:* Since she reduces her estate by the full $20,000 gift, estate taxes are reduced also when Harry and Mary die.

Example #2: Harry's estate is worth only $300,000; Mary has $2 million. They are advised to make "exemption" gifts: $300,000 Harry and $600,000 Mary. Instead, she should consider gifting $1.2 million: $600,000 with Harry's consent, and $600,000 by Mary. This approach enables her to transfer an "extra" $300,000 gift tax-free. A word of caution. Once Harry gives this consent to Mary, his $600,000 "exemption" is permanently reduced by $300,000 for transfer tax purposes.

My recommendation: Married couples should take advantage of split-gift rules when making transfers. If one spouse is ill, carefully measure the value of the assets. Then, with the help of tax counsel, the wealthier spouse should personally make gifts for both of them.

MISTAKE #11:

Not Gifting the $600,000 Lifetime "Exemption." To shift future growth outside your estate tax base, successful people should transfer $600,000 "exemptions" during their lifetimes. Sometimes, this is done gradually:

In 1997, you gave $15,000 to your son, Bill, and you transferred $5,000 to a trust for your daughter, Judy. (In each situation, there is a $5,000 taxable gift, but until the $600,000 "exemption" is fully claimed, there is no gift tax.) There are no more transfers until your death, when you pass an additional $990,000 to the family. *The result:* Your estate tax base is $1 million (previous taxable gifts of $10,000 plus $990,000), and taxes of $345,800 are computed on this amount. The calculation is completed by subtracting $192,800 - the estate tax on the $600,000 "exemption" - and your personal representative sends the IRS a check for $153,000.

To summarize, because of the unified transfer tax system,

"taxable" lifetime gifts up to $600,000 don't save any transfer taxes eventually. However, these gifts remove all growth from your estate tax base after the gift. *My recommendation:* If you are comfortable making larger gifts, give the $600,000 "exemption" as early as possible. In 10 or 20 years, a considerable amount of appreciation may be removed from your estate tax base.

MISTAKE #12:

Not Making Taxable Gifts Above the $600,000 "Exemption." Once the "exemption" is gifted, you pay gift tax on all transfers (over annual $10,000 gifts and payments of tuition and for medical expenses).

Let's assume that in 1997, you made taxable transfers of $1 million and paid the IRS $153,000 on a taxable gift of $400,000; your assets are reduced by $1,153,000 - the $1 million gift, plus tax of $153,000 on the gift of $400,000. If you live three years, however, a personal representative merely adds the $1 million transfer in 1997 to your estate tax base. *The result:* The estate "saves" the estate tax on gift taxes of $153,000 that were paid on the 1997 gifts.

My recommendation: Once the $600,000 "exemption" is gifted, it is wise to make additional taxable gifts and pay a gift tax. Once three years expires, the gift tax actually becomes a tax deduction for your estate.

CAUTION: This recommendation is strictly based on tax savings. Once again, be comfortable with the notion of making significant gifts. If not, then all of the tax savings in the law aren't enough to suggest parting with these assets. Just don't do it![4]

MISTAKE #13:

Not Paying Close Attention To The Value Of Gifts. Asset valuation is a difficult area for the tax planner. That's why the law generally protects taxpayers from extra gift taxes (on higher values) three years after a gift tax return is filed with the IRS. Unfortunately, in 1990, a Tax Court ruled that at death, when the gift is added to an estate tax base, the IRS can challenge the value of this earlier gift. Even though the Tax Recovery Act of 1997 says the IRS may no longer revalue such gifts if its statute of limitations has expired, it still is necessary to adequately disclose the information on your gift tax return. If you don't do this, expect the IRS to challenge the gift's value, if there is reason to do so.

Let's say you have $3 million in assets and made a $1 million gift in 1997. The gift tax is $153,000. You live three years, and this gift tax is removed from the estate tax base. When you die, the estate tax base is $3 million ($2 million remaining, plus the $1 million gift). If the IRS increases the gift's value in 1998 to $1.5 million, for example, the estate may pay an "extra" estate tax of $65,000. (See Exhibit 1.)

---

4 Indeed, a significant gift-giving plan can backfire. Consider the situation of billionaire Harold Simmons. Apparently, fear of a tax bill in the hundreds of millions caused his demand that daughters restructure trusts he had established for them earlier. Anyway, at least two of these daughters recently sued Harold, alleging that he set up these trusts solely for his own purposes to fend off creditors, tax collectors and former spouses. Sometimes you just can't win. Allen R. Myerson, "Daughters Do Battle With A Corporate King Lear," *The New York Times*, May 18, 1997, Sec. 3.

CAUTION: It's always possible that the IRS will revalue significant gifts that are made at any time before death. Keep documents that carefully support all values, and include them with a gift tax return to the IRS. It also helps to "hope for the best."

MISTAKE #14:

Making Taxable Gifts Of Low Basis Assets. When making $600,000 "exemption" gifts and additional taxable gifts, it's best to give tax-paid cash and property that doesn't have a low basis. Here's why:

You are about to gift $1 million (and pay a gift tax) to remove future growth from the estate tax base. If you gift low basis property, the donee must someday pay capital gains taxes on the profit at sale. If, instead, these assets are bequeathed, there is no capital gains tax on this profit because of the basis step-up at death.

For example, you have property worth $1 million that has a zero basis, and you also have a $1 million asset that has a $1 million basis. By gifting the high basis asset and passing the low basis property by bequest, heirs save a capital gains tax if they sell the low basis asset after death (and the odds are nearly 100 percent that they will make this sale).

My recommendation: When making significant gifts, gift cash or high basis property, if possible. But, discuss this matter thoroughly with advisors before doing anything.

MISTAKE #15:

Gifting Unsuitable Assets. There are always a wide range of choices when it comes to which assets should be given away. The first group of assets that makes good gifts is high basis property. These assets are cash or other "tax-paid" assets, such as municipals, corporate bonds and mutual funds (that reported most of its past profits as taxable income). The second group is growth assets that are expected to "explode," as opposed to assets which are depleting or depreciating in value over the years.

Examples Of "Growth" Gifting Include:
- Cash into life insurance premiums;
- Cash or bonds shifting into growth stocks; and
- Capital assets and partnership shares that have good accumulation potential.

Examples Of "Depleting" Or Shrinking Gift Property Include:
- Oil royalties;
- Annuities that have accumulated taxable income; and
- Capital assets that will decrease rapidly in value, such as copyrights, patent leaseholds and mineral rights.

My recommendation: Before committing to a significant gift-giving plan, be aware that the gifted assets are often property that is worth keeping. The final decision will balance a number of factors that are acquired by reading and re-reading portions of this book.

MISTAKE #16:

Gifting Life Insurance Too Late In Life. Life insurance makes an attractive gift because the gift is usually equal to the cash value, and this is usually much less than the face amount. However, the law has a penalty when policies are gifted "in contemplation of death."

Gifts of policies within three years of death "return" the full face amount to the estate tax base at death, while policies gifted more than three years before death remove face amounts from the tax base. When transferring policies, you would have to just "agree" to live three years afterwards.

My recommendation: All kidding aside, don't wait too long to give policies to trusts for heirs. Transfer these contracts early in your 50s or 60s when (a) cash values are low and (b) your anticipated life span is much longer than three years.

MISTAKE #17:

The "Unhealthy" Spouse Holds High Basis Assets. From purely a tax point of view, husbands and wives should arrange their marital assets based on age and health expectations:

Harry (age 75 and in poor health) and Mary (in good health) own most of their assets ($2 million) jointly. Since Harry is older and unhealthy, it's natural to anticipate that Mary will survive him and receive a basis step-up in one-half their assets. Harry and Mary should consider exchanging (gifting) their assets between them to obtain a preferred income tax position for the more likely survivor of them (Mary).

Naturally, it's helpful if Harry and Mary can openly discuss their mortality with each other. Then, they simply rear-

range investments so that Harry owns low(er) basis property, and Mary's assets are high(er) basis. For example, if Harry
owns $1 million (low basis) in his name, and Mary owns $1
million (high basis) in her name, Mary gains from the basis
step-up if Harry predeceases her.

CAUTION: Be aware that if you transfer property to a
donee who dies within one year of the gift, and if you receive this property back as an inheritance, a basis step-up
isn't available to the recipient. Consequently, "deathbed" gifts
of low basis property may not accomplish a basis step-up
goal.

EXHIBIT 1

HOW ESTATE TAXES ARE INCREASED WHEN A PREVIOUS GIFT IS REVALUED

	WITHOUT REVALUATION	WITH REVALUATION
Taxable Estate	$2,000,000	$2,000,000
Adjusted Taxable Gifts	1,000,000	1,500,000
Total	3,000,000	3,500,000
Tentative Tax	1,290,800	1,565,800
(Gift Tax Payable)	(153,000)	(363,000)
Tax	1,137,800	1,202,800
(Unified Credit)	(192,800)	(192,800)
Estate Tax	**$945,000** vs*	**$1,010,000**

* a $65,000 difference.

CHAPTER 5

CHARITABLE TAX PLANNING:
MAKING BENEVOLENCE A WIN-WIN PROPOSITION

C an charitable contributions "make money" for the donor? Can sophisticated charitable tax planning work for everyone? Is there a wrong way to donate to charities? In this chapter, we'll consider questions such as these that keep professionals buzzing at tax conferences. Be aware, however, that some of this information is quite technical. You'll want to review this more than once before sharing it with your advisors.

Over the years, you've probably developed your own personal view on philanthropy. If this policy is effective, you know that good things come back to donors - and keep coming, when contributions are part of a well-crafted tax plan. But if your benevolence has backfired, you may feel pessimistic about making additional donations. No need to worry. The strategies outlined ahead will make gifting to charities a win-win proposition. There's no reason why a donor can't benefit, when sharing wealth with others less fortunate! Let's look at some tax planning strategies first:

A FEW BASIC CHARITABLE TAX PLANNING STRATEGIES

The current Tax Code promotes gifting by providing several interesting tax planning opportunities. To refresh your memory, here are some of the best:

1. For gifts made *directly* to public charities, there are tax deductions up to 50 percent of adjusted gross income (AGI) for gifts of cash, and up to 30 percent of AGI for gifts of capital assets, real estate, stocks, etc.

2. There are tax deductions for gifts of capital assets without having to first pay taxes on built-in capital gains.[1] Let's

---

1 On Sept. 18, 1997, Ted Turner, Vice Chairman of Time Warner, Inc. said in a Larry King CNN interview that he is creating a foundation to fund United Nations programs. He'll gift $100 million of Time Warner stock annually for 10 years to this new foundation. "Turner's $1 billion gift," Reuter, *Rocky Mountain News*, Sept. 19, 1997, p. 2A. Notice that Mr. Turner avoids a capital gains tax on the appreciation in his stock, and he obtains an income tax deduction on the entire value of his contribution. In order to fully use this deduction (probably at the rate of 20 per cent of his AGI), he spreads a $1 billion gift over a 10-year period. See also Elliot Blair Smith, "Ted's Excellent Donation, When Does a $1 Billion Gift Turn Into a $100 Million Gain?," *USA Today*, Sept. 23, 1997. Ted Turner also teaches us how to use *collars* to assure his commitment to charity. Greg Ip, "Collars Give Insiders Way To Cut Risk," *The Wall Street Journal*, Sept. 17, 1997, p. C1. This relatively obscure investment strategy is the simultaneous (a) sale of a call, an option to buy stocks in the future at a set price, and (b) purchase of a put, an option to sell these securities at another set price. See Richard W. Duff, "Charitable Contributions, Collars, and Covered Calls in Wealth Preservation," *Journal of Financial Planning*, Dec., 1997. Finally, he will probably control his foundation at least indirectly—and Time Warner may even benefit from all of the publicity. The *bottom line*: As Ted Turner does good works, he shows us how to make charitable giving a win-win proposition. In effect, he tells all who can to follow his example and do the same.

say your business owns real estate worth $100,000, and the basis is zero. A charitable contribution of this property could net a full tax deduction of $100,000. If you place this property in a qualified retirement plan instead, there is a tax deduction, but you'd have to pay a capital gains tax of say $20,000 (at a 20 percent rate).

3. You can make a gift now (or bequest later) that provides an income for the life of one or more persons. One example is a charitable gift annuity. Another is a gift to a charitable remainder trust (CRT), where you and your spouse keep an income and the remainder eventually passes to a charity (See Illustration #1). *The good news:* If you wish to be the trustee of this trust, this is permitted in most instances.

4. You can make gifts (or bequests) for a specific term, and keep the remainder for an heir. For example, a gift to a charitable lead trust (CLT) allows a charity to get cash flow for a specified number of years, and the remainder is returned to family after this term.

5. It may be possible to neutralize income or capital gains tax on most any source of income when it is offset by charitable contributions that involve a life insurance contract. This plan not only produces a substantial endowment for your favorite charity, but it can potentially provide your family access to cash flow from the policy and even liquidity for your estate taxes.[2]

---

2 One of these arrangements is referred to as a Charitable Legacy Plan (CLP), a trademark of InsMark, Inc. 2274 Camino Ramon, San Ramon, CA 94583. It isn't often that new charitable planning programs (like CLPs) are presented to the public in an imaginative way. Consequently, I've included material on the Charitable Legacy

These five tips are examples of how the tax law permits you to win and do good at the same time. When you understand the concepts, it's relatively easy to put them into practice. Nonetheless, a lot can go wrong when a charitable plan is implemented (or even when one is being considered). Let's review some of these pitfalls next.

CHARITABLE TAX PLANNING TRAPS AND PITFALLS

ERROR # 1:

Your Charitable Financial Plan Is Too Complicated. Many good charitable gifting ideas aren't implemented because the plan is too complicated with one confusing detail after another. *The result:* Nothing is done, because when there is too much to learn, it's just easier not to bother. It may even seem too good to be true!

My recommendation: Ask an advisor to strip away the financial details. All you want to know are: (1) the tax benefits, (2) the financial consequences to family and charity, and (3) a comparison of where everyone stands if (a) the plan is implemented or (b) it is not! Then, you'll make a decision based on the facts, as well as your philanthropic intentions.

Plan at the end of this chapter. Much of it is taken from copyrighted material, with the approval of InsMark and Bob Ritter, its creative president. The text also tells how you can get more details about CLP. A word of caution: As this is written in 1998, there is no direct IRS authority on CLP. Until there is a case or ruling, I recommend that you work closely with tax and financial counsel before implementing this arrangement. Be flexible. Expect to hear disadvantages as well as the advantages.

ERROR # 2:

You Don't Have A Charitable Plan At All. Those who haven't investigated a philanthropic gifting strategy, have really missed some interesting possibilities. For instance, my favorite is a charitable remainder trust (CRT) that is arranged for your personal benefit. (It belongs to a charity later.) A well-arranged charitable tax plan involving a charitable remainder trust should permit you:

·   at least a **partial tax deduction** for most contributions;

·   **avoidance of all taxes** on trust investment earnings and profits;

·   a **regular income** to you for at least your life span (and perhaps for your heirs, as well), and some **flexibility** in choosing when to take most distributions;

·   personal **control** over most investment decisions; and

·   the ability to **name the actual charity** recipient later.

Does this sound too good to be true? Well, all of this and more is possible. In other words, creative charitable tax planning can be the solution to most tax and financial worries. Gifts always come back; our tax law is just waiting for a receptive donor to use it. It's just a matter of knowing the secrets of how to do this.

ERROR # 3:

You Don't Have A Good Charitable Tax Plan. A profitable charitable plan requires considerable time and effort, and it's easy to make a mistake. Unfortunately, our philan-

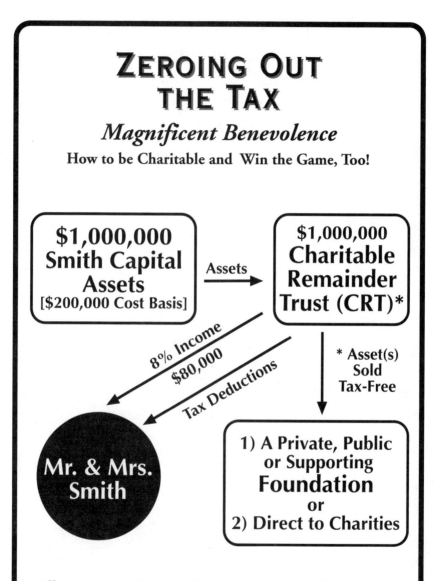

ZEROING OUT THE TAX

Magnificent Benevolence

How to be Charitable and Win the Game, Too!

$1,000,000 Smith Capital Assets
[$200,000 Cost Basis]

Assets →

$1,000,000 Charitable Remainder Trust (CRT)*

8% Income $80,000

Tax Deductions

* Asset(s) Sold Tax-Free

Mr. & Mrs. Smith

1) A Private, Public or Supporting **Foundation**
or
2) Direct to Charities

Illustration 1: By transferring appreciated assets to a charitable remainder trust (CRT), they can be sold tax-free. There are tax deductions and more cash flow. The assets pass to a tax qualified charity(ies) after the non-charitable beneficiaries dies.

thropic role models sometimes create below-average charitable arrangements.[3] In fact, there is much to learn from the errors of others. The truth is that without a truly sound plan, you're probably better off without one at all.

Here are two examples of what not to do:

Warren Buffet's Plan

First, don't use Warren Buffet's alleged charitable estate plan as a model. According to author-lawyer, William Zabel (and his reference to the October 1994 Forbes 400), multi-billionaire Warren Buffet bequeaths essentially his entire estate directly to his estranged spouse, Susan. By an "oral agreement" she'll then gift or bequeath this property to Mr. Buffet's private foundation at a later date.[4]

Mr. Buffet has essentially allowed Susan to leave her inheritance to anyone she chooses. It's even possible to imagine a lawsuit between Mr. Buffet's foundation and Susan or her heirs, in which the chief argument will be whether the oral agreement is enforceable. Finally, if Susan chooses to make a non-charitable bequest instead, the IRS will surely take a 55 percent estate tax and this could get expensive.

My recommendation: If Warren and Susan are still mar-

---

3 Apparently, Jack Kent Cooke bequeathed his interest in the Washington Redskins and many other holdings to the Jack Kent Cooke Foundation. "Cooke Family Sells Los Angeles Paper, " from News Services, *The Washington Post*, Dec. 5, 1997, p. G10. While this is a major charitable gift, it is "below average" in the sense that before he died, he eliminated his wife, Marlene, from his will. Now she is claiming one-third of Cooke's $500 million to $825 million estate. See Chapter 8, footnote 17; if successful, her share (and possibly estate taxes equal to her inheritance) could cancel out much of his philanthropy. Just imagine how a little creative planning and a life insurance policy would have improved this situation for everyone involved.

4 See William Zabel, *The Rich Die Richer and You Can Too,* (Morrow, 1995), p. ix.

ried, he can leave her a qualified terminable interest property (QTIP) trust, which provides her with lifetime income, with his foundation receiving the remainder of the estate at her death. There are no estate taxes, and the outcome is completely predictable.

Jacqueline Onassis' Plan

Jacqueline Onassis' charitable estate plan is also problematic. It is widely reported that the estate of Jacqueline Onassis was worth as much as $100 million and that she left the bulk of it to a charitable lead annuity trust (CLAT).[5] There wouldn't be any estate taxes, and her grandchildren would receive the remainder 24 years after her death. The press acclaimed this as an excellent charitable estate plan.

But apparently the arrangement began unraveling in 1996. First, many of her valuable possessions were sold in April by Sotheby's to pay some unexpected estate taxes.[6] Then in 1997 the IRS entered, and it questioned whether sale profits should be taxed as capital gains (28 percent), or as an increase in the estate value (55 percent) instead because their value on the estate tax return is too low.

Finally, it became clear that the charitable trust (called the C & J Foundation) was subject to the approval of Mrs. Onassis' children, Caroline and John. According to the *New York Times*,[7] executors now confirm that this trust no longer exists because the children want to pay the taxes and keep

---

5 *Ibid.*, pp. 161-162.

6 "Jackie's Own," *People Magazine*, Jan. 8, 1996, p. 118.

7 David Cay Johnston, "Jacqueline Onassis' Estate Worth Less Than Estimated," *The New York Times*, Dec. 21, 1996.

the rest for themselves.[8]

I believe we'll hear more about the charitable intentions of Jacqueline Onassis and her family. The sad part is how much scrutiny this matter has received. (Her will is even available on the Internet.) This should be a private affair for her family to resolve. *My recommendation:* To assure privacy in charitable affairs, begin a plan while you're alive; then, leave specific instructions in a revocable living trust to perpetuate everything after your death.[9]

ERROR # 4:

Not Arranging An Estate Tax-Free Charitable Plan. Sometimes, successful persons don't want a liquidity plan that pays estate taxes; they just want to help others, be left alone, and not pay any transfer taxes at death.[10] Consider, for instance, what a philanthropist might do with goals of

---

8 Mrs. Onassis actually left most of her estate to John and Caroline with a provision that they could *disclaim* in favor of the C & J Foundation. If John and Caroline didn't file this disclaimer, they would have to create the C & J Foundation and make the charitable gift personally.

9 Consider the story of Charles Feeney who creates a chain of successful duty-free shops (DFS Group) at airports. He then donates most of a large fortune to his foundations, anonymously. In 1997, these foundations are worth billions and Mr. Feeney lives quietly and modestly. According to Donald Kaul, "Estate of Poor Little Rich Girl; Doris Duke Provides Rich Pickings for Legal Vultures," Tribune Media Service, *The Sacramento Bee*, Feb. 3, 1997, p. B7, this unpretentious philanthropist (Mr. Feeney) says: "People of substantial wealth potentially create problems for future generations unless they themselves accept responsibility to use their wealth during the lifetime to help worthwhile causes." What a magnificent statement by such a generous and kind man! Also, see Maureen Dowd, "A billionaire gives it away," *Austin American-Statesman*, Nov. 28, 1997, p. A23.

10 According to Dana Wechsler and Dyan Machan, "The Disinheritors," *Forbes*, May 19, 1997, the really super-rich are more charitable than ever. For instance,

privacy, charity and legitimate estate tax avoidance. He or she might:

· Establish a charitable trust and a personal revocable living trust (RLT) during his or her lifetime;

· Leave a significant charitable gift at death from the RLT, and avoid all estate taxes;

· Discourage attacks on this arrangement by providing forfeitures if inheritors attack the overall plan; or

· Have an irrevocable trust acquire tax-free substantial life insurance on the donor's life to "replace" all or some of her charitable gifts. (See Illustration #2.)

Philanthropic motives are strengthened by the charitable trust, and the RLT assures privacy. Estate taxes are eliminated or reduced by the charitable bequest, and finally, the gift or bequest is replaced with exactly the amount of life insurance desired. This may truly be the "perfect" estate plan.

Tips When Considering a Personal CRT

Trusts and Estates and *Estate Planning Magazine* are publications that most wealth preservation professionals read regularly. In nearly every issue, there are updates and articles to make it clear that just about everyone can benefit by establishing a charitable tax planning strategy.

In fact, entire articles and seminars are devoted exclusively to charitable remainder trusts (CRTs) as the cornerstone to

Microsoft founder, William Henry Gates, III, will give $10 million to each of his children with the rest to charity; Home Depot Chairman, Bernard Marcus will leave $850 million in stock to the Marcus Foundation; and David Packard, co-founder of Hewlett-Packard, who died in 1996, gave away more than $5 billion before his death.

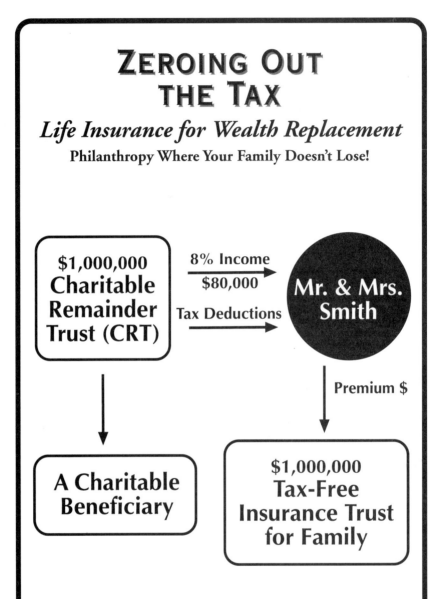

ZEROING OUT THE TAX

Life Insurance for Wealth Replacement
Philanthropy Where Your Family Doesn't Lose!

$1,000,000 Charitable Remainder Trust (CRT)

8% Income
$80,000 →

Tax Deductions →

Mr. & Mrs. Smith

Premium $

A Charitable Beneficiary

$1,000,000 Tax-Free Insurance Trust for Family

Illustration 2: When you establish a Wealth Replacement insurance trust insuring lives of the non-charitable beneficiaries of the CRT, your family isn't left out.

a good estate plan.[11] Some say you don't even have to be charitable to use them effectively. If you really want to avoid taxes as you do good works for others, below are twelve pointers you need to know when considering a CRT for yourself and family:

1. The donor always receives a tax deduction for contributions. The deductible amount increases with your age and is equal to the remainder portion a charity receives after a trust beneficiary(ies) dies. For example, if the present value of an income interest is 65 percent of the gift, the deductible remainder value is 35 percent.[12]

2. A deduction is claimed currently of up to 30 percent of your Adjusted Gross Income (AGI). If it isn't used fully this year, any balance can be claimed on your next five tax returns.

3. These are created as tax-exempt trusts: As long as a CRT is tax-exempt, it doesn't pay tax on investment income or capital gains from sales of appreciated property. It is tax-exempt if the trust avoids having business income unrelated to its exempt purpose.

4. You can usually be trustee of your own trust. It's advisable to select another trustee, however, when a CRT sells stock in a closely-held business, land or other hard-to-value

11 If you are considering the sale of real estate, securities or even a family business, I recommend considering the CRT alternative. At the end of this chapter there is a CRT analysis prepared by Vaughn Henry. If you contact him, mention this book.

12 Let's say you gift $100,000 to a CRT and retain an $8,000 annual income for your life expectancy which is 15 years—a total of $120,000. Today's (present) value of these expected payments is about $65,000. Consequently, the value of the remainder is $35,000.

assets. It's also possible to make a charity trustee. *My recommendation:* Ask a personal advisor what is best for you.

5. Its assets are sheltered from your judgment creditors. It may be possible to protect your CRT income interest as well, if the trust is located in a foreign country.

6. There is no estate tax if a spouse becomes the trust beneficiary at your death. Note that your spouse must be named specifically in the trust document.

7. If a child becomes the beneficiary after a parent's death, there is a calculation to determine the charity's portion of the trust value at that time. After subtracting the remainder, the present value of a child's life income share is a taxable transfer which is included in the parent's estate tax base at that time.

8. Sometimes it's best to put a "toe in the water" first by gifting a small amount of money to a CRT. Then, make a much larger gift of an appreciated asset later when you are completely comfortable with the arrangement. If you take this approach, the trust must be a unitrust (CRUT) which pays a percentage of its assets as an income. An annuity trust (CRAT) pays a specific amount.

9. If desired, in most cases an eventual charitable remainder can be selected later by a non-charitable beneficiary. (If a family foundation *may* be a charitable beneficiary, the donor's tax deduction for most trust contributions is limited to basis.) Keep in mind, however, that if you name the charity irrevocable beneficiary, it may show appreciation by paying for the preparation and administration of the trust. You'll

never know until you ask.

10. To replace assets donated through CRTs to charities, create trusts that acquire insurance on your life. The proceeds "replace" wealth that will someday belong to a charity

11. There are certain assets that generally aren't suitable for a CRT. For example, do not contribute mortgaged real estate or S corporation stock before checking with a tax lawyer.

12. Finally, be aware of a "surprise" portion of the Taxpayer Relief Act of 1997, which disqualifies charitable deductions for any CRT were the remainder interest is less than 10 percent. As a practical matter, this may preclude the use of these trusts by persons younger than age 35.

Since 1969, charitable remainder trusts have clearly been available for all taxpayers. The tax law actually encourages everyone to use them. Yet, there are some unique traps that await those who have (or should have) a CRT. Let's review a few:

TRAPS AND PITFALLS COMMON TO CRT PLANNING

ERROR # 1:

Selling Any Appreciated Assets And Paying Capital Gains Taxes. Some say it's a mistake to ever pay a capital gains tax, since it's possible to avoid all taxes on the appreciation of property by simply donating it before making a sale.

For instance, you establish a charitable remainder unitrust (CRUT) with a modest $1,000 contribution of cash. Then, you place real estate in this trust. It locates a buyer and sells its property tax-free. Later, you gift marketable securities to the trust, and they are sold tax-free. Eventually, you donate a business (and even a residence), and these are also sold without a capital gains tax.

In other words, you needn't ever pay a capital gains tax if you contribute appreciated property before you sell it. Imagine tax savings that are possible just by having a CRT available for the capital assets you own personally. And once this trust sells an appreciated asset, future investment earnings and profits are also protected from taxes - only the payment made to you each year is taxable. CRTs seem almost too good to be true, but the law blesses them. You just have to be willing to eventually benefit a favorite charity. *CAUTION:* Don't arrange a sale before contributing an asset to the trust.

My recommendation: Avoid the mistake of paying capital gains taxes (and taxes on investment income). Establish a charitable remainder trust in your late 30s or 40s. And then enjoy the tax and financial advantages for years (and even generations) to come.

ERROR # 2:

Taking Too Much From A CRT. When establishing a CRT, a rate of payment is selected that the trust must distribute until a remainder is paid to charity. It's natural, therefore, to choose a rate much higher than the 5 percent minimum required by law, but this can be a poor planning decision.

Let's assume a $100,000 10 percent charitable remainder unitrust earns exactly 10 percent annually at the end of the year, and this is distributed. *The result:* The value of the trust remains the same at $100,000, and there is no opportunity for tax deferral. If, instead, this is a 5 percent trust, it appreciates tax-free by a net 5 percent (10 percent less the 5 percent payout) annually; after 25 years, there is $338,000 in the trust, and it is still paying 5 percent, or $16,900 that year.

My recommendation: In most cases, you'll benefit long-range by selecting a lower percentage income and gaining from tax-free deferral within the trust.

ERROR # 3:

Foregoing A "NIMCRUT" CRT. There is a special CRT that primarily benefits those who establish these trusts early in life. You create a charitable remainder unitrust that distributes, say, 5 percent annually, but the payment is reduced if the trust's income is less. This trust arranges its investments (in growth stocks or undeveloped real estate) that pay merely a "token" income as they appreciate in the trust. The income shortfall is credited to a "makeup" account for payment at a later date. Referred to as a NIMCRUT (Net Income With Makeup Charitable Remainder Unitrust), it offers the optimum in tax-deferral.

Let's say you create a $100,000 5 percent NIMCRUT,

and it earns zero income over a 30-year period. If it has an 8 percent growth rate during this time, it will build to $1 million, and you'll eventually be a CRT "millionaire" through the magic of tax-deferral. Then, this trust switches to an 8 percent income investment and distributes the $900,000 makeup account gradually as it makes its regular 5 percent payment. You'll receive a 5 percent payment of $50,000 (5 percent x $1 million), plus an additional 3 percent distribution of $27,000 from the makeup account — for a total of $77,000 annually.

My recommendation: Although NIMCRUTs offer flexibility and some exciting tax planning opportunities, I suggest caution when it comes to creating this type of trust. "Crunch the numbers" carefully, and thoroughly discuss the results with your legal and financial advisors.

CAUTION: A makeup account is forfeited (to charity) if it isn't distributed during the lifetime(s) of a non-charitable beneficiary. If this concerns you, one possibility is to include family as additional trust beneficiaries. By "borrowing" their life spans, you'll increase the possibility that a large makeup account is fully payable before the remainder goes to charity.

ERROR # 4:

Using A "Spigot" NIMCRUT. Sometimes, the IRS says it's possible to create too much of a good thing. Creative planners have formed NIMCRUTs that invest in annuities, zero coupon bonds (zeros), as well as capital property. These trusts have a special twist, however. They define the growth or "build-up" on investments as income only when the trust surrenders or withdraws (annuities), liquidates (zeros at the maturity date), or sells (capital assets).

The objective is to permit a NIMCRUT to accumulate on a tax-deferred basis, but allow for the trust to pay out tax-deferred build-up all at once someday in the future. ***CAUTION:*** The IRS has distributed material to its agents criticizing these charitable trusts.[13] It's my opinion that much of the reasoning is faulty. However, if an advisor recommends a NIMCRUT, review it carefully because the IRS may take a position against some of the benefits being promised.

ERROR # 5:

Terminating A CRT Too Soon. Normally, a donor establishes a CRT for his or her lifetime, a one-lifetime trust. If a spouse is named as successor beneficiary, it is a two-lifetime trust. Either way, there is a charitable deduction for the remainder value, and no estate tax as trust assets eventually pass at the "second death" to your charity. In a two-lifetime trust, the charity waits longer to receive the remainder. Therefore, charitable income tax deductions for contributions to these CRTs are always less than for one-lifetime trusts.

Unfortunately, it's not well-known that CRTs can be continued for two, three or even four lifetimes. Yet, in many cases, this is exactly the best approach.

The most interesting benefit of CRTs is potential tax-

---

13 See *Chapter K of the 1996 (For FY 1997) Exempt Organizations Continuing Professional Education Technical Instruction Program Textbook.*

deferral over a long period of time. Imagine maintaining this feature for a child or even a grandchild for years to come. This may add 25-50 more years of tax-deferred investing for your family.

CAUTION: When third and fourth-lifetime beneficiaries are added in a trust, keep in mind that a charity waits even longer to receive its assets. There is a reduced charitable income tax deduction, but this minor disadvantage is usually offset by prolonged tax-deferral for family. This value (equal to lifetime income) is also included in the estate tax base when it passes from parent to child, and there may be a generation-skipping transfer too if it passes from child to grandchild.

My recommendation: If you set up a two, three or four-lifetime trust, it cannot pay any transfer taxes your family will incur. It's best therefore, to maintain insurance outside the trust as a source of estate tax liquidity.

SPECIAL PLANNING MISTAKES TO AVOID

MISTAKE # 1:

Gifting A Deferred Annuity Policy Acquired After April 22, 1987, To Charity. Commercial annuities are popular because they defer taxes on interest credited by the insurer. However, annuity policies do not make an attractive gift. Here's why: You place $100,000 in an annuity policy, and assume it is currently worth $250,000. Someone says, "Donate this to charity and deduct $250,000 against your income taxes." The pitfall is, since you pay income taxes on the *profit* when you give an annuity, you won't have the annuity policy as a source of cash for the tax. Therefore, a commercial annuity is not a good asset to use as a charitable gift.

My recommendation: It may be more attractive to make a charitable bequest of this annuity at death. The full value should be deductible against your estate tax base, and the accumulated profit won't be added to the estate's taxable income.

MISTAKE # 2:

Bequeathing The Wrong Asset To Charity. It's best to seek professional advice regarding which assets are best suited for charitable gifting. The wrong choice is a tax disaster.

For example: You have assets that bring your estate tax base to $3 million. They include a $500,000 pension account and land worth $500,000. Which asset should you bequeath to charity and which should you leave to family?

My recommendation: Since a pension account of $500,000 may be worth only about $150,000 for your family after both estate and income taxes are subtracted, give this to charity. Then leave the real estate to your family. Since land receives a basis step-up, it should be worth more like $250,000 net after merely a 50 percent estate tax is subtracted.

MISTAKE # 3:

Making Pre-Arranged Charitable Gifts. There is a long-standing battle between the IRS, donors and charities (especially certain charitable remainder trusts) regarding pre-arranged sales of appreciated assets. If the IRS wins the battle, you pay tax on any profit from the sale, which could put your entire plan in jeopardy.

For example: Joe Higgins gifts appreciated real estate, but he has made a contract (before the gift) to sell this land to Mary Johnson. The result: Joe is taxed on the capital gains because the IRS says the charitable trust is merely acting as his agent.

Tax law is especially sensitive to such matters[14] as: (a) pre-arranged sales, (b) the anticipatory assignment of profit on the sale proceeds, (c) "side" agreements with CRTs or charities, and (d) self-dealing, where a donor gains personal advantages aside from normal charitable tax deductions. For the most part, the rules are based on common sense, but there are some traps for the unwary.

My recommendation: If your charitable gift planning becomes at all complicated, it's best to seek competent legal advice and follow the law to the letter.

MISTAKE # 4:

Overlooking The Benefits Of Charitable Lead Trusts (CLTs). The flip side of the more popular charitable remainder trust is a charitable lead trust (CLT) which gives charity the leading income interest for a period of time; then the

---

14 In 1997, the IRS won an interesting case where, unfortunately, a taxpayer had to pay capital gains taxes on a gift to charity of Company A appreciated stock. Company B had agreed earlier to purchase Company A shares if 85 percent of Company A shareholders agreed to sell. See *Michael Ferguson V. Comm.,* 108 T.C. No. 14 (April 28, 1997).

remainder belongs to others such as the donor's heirs. The charity's interest is either a fixed amount (annuity) or a set percentage (unitrust) payment. The remainder is either paid directly to family or held in a trust for their benefit.

Jacqueline Onassis specified that her CLT would pay a fixed annuity (8 percent of an initial gift) to the C & J Foundation - for 24 years. The remainder would "skip" her children for heirs in a generation-skipping (GS) trust to terminate no later than "21 years after the death of the last to die of the descendants of my former father-in-law, Joseph P. Kennedy, who were in being at the time of my death."[15] After 24 years, her heirs would incur a 55 percent GS tax when they received payments from the trust. (Note: If this were a unitrust, it might be arranged to avoid a GS tax.) Although it appears Mrs. Onassis' charity won't become effective, she gives us a blueprint for what may be done. Unfortunately, until recently, CLTs have frequently been overlooked.

What if you really want to make a significant bequest to charity, but you don't want to exclude your grandchildren from their inheritance? One option is to make a bequest to a private foundation that benefits charity perpetually. However, while heirs can receive salaries for managing this property, it still belongs solely to the foundation. Instead, you can employ the approach outlined by Mrs. Onassis. Create a CLT interest equal to the value of trust principal, and give a remainder to family. Here's an example of the tax and fi-

---

15 See The Last Will and Testament of Jacqueline Kennedy Onassis, Article Fifth B.

nancial math:

Let's say you bequeath a $1 million estate to an 8 percent charitable lead annuity trust that pays your charity an 8 percent annual amount for 24 years. If the IRS 7520 rate is 6 percent, the present value of this interest is also nearly $1 million. *The result:* The charitable income interest is an estate tax deduction; estate taxes are eliminated, and heirs receive their $1 million inheritance 24 years after your death. If annual earnings exceed 8 percent ($80,000) paid to charity, they are taxable to the trust, and the net appreciation belongs to your family.

Most experts agree that CLTs work best when a charitably-motivated donor has sizable wealth. A fixed payment annuity trust provides more for family if trust earnings exceed the payout rate. If the trust earns less, a variable payout unitrust is preferable.

My recommendation: Since the calculations are complicated, just make sure financial projections are conservative when illustrating your family's financial position. Although, this plan can significantly benefit charity and provide even more for future generations, it all depends on the 7520 rate, a payout rate, trust earnings and an overall estate plan. If you're philanthropic, don't overlook them in your charitable program.

MISTAKE # 5:

Becoming An Uninsured Fiduciary-Charitable Contributor. If you're a dedicated philanthropist, a non-profit organization may ask for your time and energy as a board member, officer or trustee. ***CAUTION:*** You'll be expected to perform at a standard higher than directors and officers of a profit-making company. For example, if someone sues you for (a) a breach of care or loyalty, (b) personal or financial loss, or (c) the violation of laws or rules, most personal liability insurance programs don't cover duties performed in a fiduciary capacity.

My recommendation: Before accepting a position of trust with a charitable organization, ask it to investigate directors' and officers' insurance that will fully cover all of your activities for them. If coverage is available, make it a condition of your employment.

MISTAKE # 6:

Not Investigating A Charity's Financial Situation. Occasionally, there are situations where philanthropy literally runs amuck. Take the situation of New Era Philanthropy (1989-1995), and its founder and president, John G. Bennett, Jr. This organization duped many donors by simply promising that "anonymous philanthropists" would match donations that it received. There were no such persons, and this classic Ponzi scheme eventually backfired to the dismay of newer investors who lost everything.[16]

My recommendation: There can be arrangements that are

16 Charles D. Fox, IV and Benetta Y. Park, "How Fiduciaries Can Avoid Another New Era Philanthropy Debacle," *Trusts and Estate Magazine,* May, 1997, pp. 26-27. As Mr. Bennett put it on Sept. 16, 1997, in his swindling trial—"I'm just very, very bad at handling money"—*The Denver Post,* Sept. 21, 1997, p. K3. On September 22nd, John Bennett was sentenced to a long prison term. Dinah Washington, "Charity scam operator, 60, given 12-year prison term," Associated Press, *Rocky Mountain News,* Sept. 23, 1997.

"too good to be true." If you are approached with a charitable plan that meets this definition, get a second opinion before you buy-in. If there are questions about the charity, itself, ask for (1) an audited financial statement, (2) proof of state registration as an exempt organization, and (3) referrals to long-standing contributors.

THE CHARITABLE LEGACY PLAN

(A Trademark Of Insmark Insurance Services)[17]

The CLP technique is one of the most flexible of all the charitable giving strategies.

What it is and how it works: A Charitable Legacy Plan (CLP) is a financial strategy used by those wanting to accumulate cash and/or estate assets for family members (possibly including themselves) on a tax favored basis using income tax deductible funding. (See Illustrations #3 and #4.)

CLP involves the purchase of a life insurance policy that is shared with a charitable organization. The charity's share consists of part of the death benefit for a specified term of years – usually not longer than the life expectancy of the insured. The charity pays a term-type premium for its death benefit interest. The policyowner - perhaps an irrevocable life insurance trust (ILIT) created by the insured – pays any balance of the premiums, owns the policy cash values, and is the beneficiary of the remaining death benefit.

So as not to leave the charity with an "empty bag" the

[17]This information is adapted with the permission of Insmark from its copyrighted material.

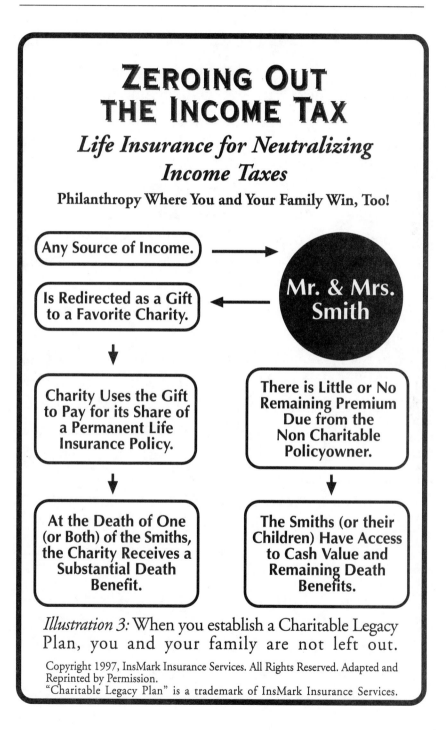

ZEROING OUT THE INCOME TAX

Life Insurance for Neutralizing Income Taxes

Philanthropy Where You and Your Family Win, Too!

Any Source of Income. → **Mr. & Mrs. Smith**

Is Redirected as a Gift to a Favorite Charity. ←

Charity Uses the Gift to Pay for its Share of a Permanent Life Insurance Policy.

There is Little or No Remaining Premium Due from the Non Charitable Policyowner.

At the Death of One (or Both) of the Smiths, the Charity Receives a Substantial Death Benefit.

The Smiths (or their Children) Have Access to Cash Value and Remaining Death Benefits.

Illustration 3: When you establish a Charitable Legacy Plan, you and your family are not left out.

agreement between the charity and policy owner provides the charity with a life-long extended death benefit interest in the policy. The charity owes no premiums for this extension.

An interested charitable donor (the insured, insured's spouse, family member, business entity, etc.) makes a contribution to the charity. The donation is an unrestricted cash gift. For the donation to be tax deductible, there must be no agreement, written or unwritten, between the donor and the charity which requires the charity to use it for premium payment. The charity will probably use the donation to pay for its share, but there must be no obligation to do this.

Benefits to the policy owner: Policy cash values that belong to the ILIT may be accessed via income tax free loans and distributed to family members (including a non-insured spouse). (See chapters 9, 10 and 11.) At the insured's death, policy benefits are paid which can produce income streams for family members (including a surviving spouse) or liquidity to help offset wealth transfer taxes.

Benefits to the charity: The charity is assured of a substantial death benefit to enhance the funding for its mission while incurring little or no fundraising costs to secure the gift.

Benefits to the charitable donor: The charitable donor takes comfort in providing a substantial gift to a worthy cause. He or she is also eligible for an income tax deduction for the contribution to the charity – subject to the donor's contribution limitations.

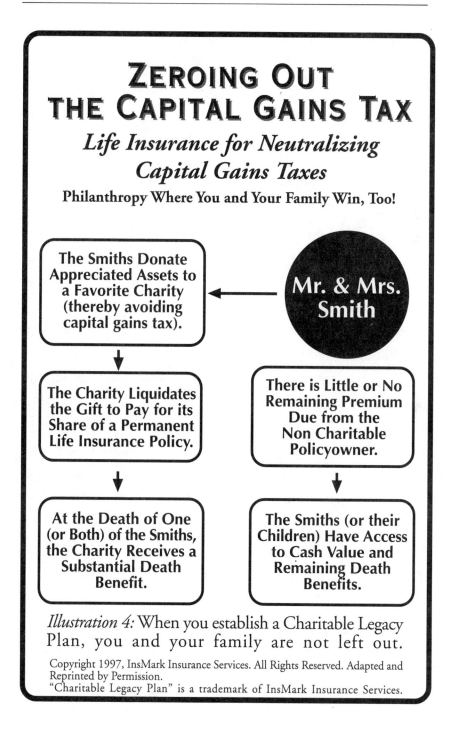

ZEROING OUT
THE CAPITAL GAINS TAX

Life Insurance for Neutralizing
Capital Gains Taxes

Philanthropy Where You and Your Family Win, Too!

The Smiths Donate Appreciated Assets to a Favorite Charity (thereby avoiding capital gains tax). ← **Mr. & Mrs. Smith**

The Charity Liquidates the Gift to Pay for its Share of a Permanent Life Insurance Policy.

There is Little or No Remaining Premium Due from the Non Charitable Policyowner.

At the Death of One (or Both) of the Smiths, the Charity Receives a Substantial Death Benefit.

The Smiths (or their Children) Have Access to Cash Value and Remaining Death Benefits.

Illustration 4: When you establish a Charitable Legacy Plan, you and your family are not left out.

Additional information: The Charitable Legacy Plan is available from a select group of individuals licensed by InsMark, Inc., a financial services company and the creator of the concept. For more information or an introduction to a licensee near you, visit the CLP Home Page available from Insmark's Internet site at: http://www.insmark.com.

A word of caution: Like many financial transactions, CLP is not specifically mentioned in tax law; however, it is a concept based on sound policy sharing principles, and InsMark licensees can provide substantial legal and tax research that supports this position.

The insurance policy sharing principles used with CLP do have precedent in the private sector. Known as "private" split dollar plans, they have a long history of use. Moreover, the IRS has recently issued several favorable letter rulings regarding such plans, and most commentators are comfortable with such policy sharing arrangements. It is possible, however, that some advisers may find variations of the CLP too aggressive for some estate owners. Clearly, this type of creative tax planning should be reviewed carefully by an attorney to determine its suitability for your specific circumstances.

A SUMMARY OF THE KEY FEATURES OF A CHARITABLE LEGACY PLAN (CLP)

· Tax deductible funding for any individual or entity;
· A substantial life insurance death benefit for family and charity;

- Possible *access* to tax-free cash flow by the non-charitable policyowner;

- No government tax qualified plan limitations or IRS pre-approval required;

- Low setup and maintenance costs;

- Appreciated stock can be used for the charitable contribution to avoid a capital gains tax;

- Possible creditor protection for family wealth if the policy owner is an irrevocable life insurance trust (ILIT), family limited partnership (FLP), or limited liability company (LLC);

- Death benefits may be completely free of estate taxes if the policy owner is an ILIT or adult child;

- Death benefits may be partially free of estate taxes if the policy owner is an FLP or LLC and gifting of partnership interests is underway; and

- If an ILIT or adult child is a policyowner, the plan may not require full use of annual gift exclusions, unified credit transfers, or generation skipping exemptions for premiums dedicated to the policy.

THE CRT ALTERNATIVE[1]

John and Betsy Moore, ages 62 and 59, have an 80 acre parcel of ground that has been used primarily for corn and soybean production for their family farm. Recently, they have been offered a price based on a square footage figure for their land, acreage that they bought years ago for $500/acre. Since the Moore's children are no longer active on the farm, the questions about preserving value and using assets to provide for a retirement have popped up. The Moore's view this as an opportunity to create retirement security, since neither managed to set aside much in their IRAs. As they reviewed the tax liability with their accountant, he suggested that they call me to run a sample scenario* and compare what would happen if they kept the land and continued to farm it, or sold it and paid the tax, reinvesting the balance, or transferred it to a CRT. The following chart seems self-explanatory, and they decided it made more sense to utilize the CRT as a retirement and tax planning tool and keep their assets in the community. In this case, they chose to fund a local hospital, a nursing home and a college in a nearby town, rather than let the IRS collect unnecessary tax and have the funds redirected to other nonlocal causes.

*   Hypothetical evaluations are provided as a professional courtesy to members of the estate planning community. Feel free to call for suggestions.

**   Insurance premium of $25,028 for duration of joint life expectancy was used so there would be no difference between options B and C in the net cash flow ($775,867) was removed from option C cash flow to fund WRT. Policy used was a variable universal type survivor life policy with investment options at 10% like alternative investment assumptions. Funded with Crummey gifts to LIT. All investment returns are hypothetical with no guarantee of future performance.

***   Value to family does not include the appreciated value of the charitable gift to family philanthropic interest.

(1) Prepared by Vaughn Henry, Henry & Associates, Springfield, Il.

Moore Farm CRT Strategy	Keep Asset at Work and Pass to Heirs (A)	Sell Asset and Reinvest the Balance (B)	Gift Asset to CRT and Reinvest (C)
Fair market Value of 80 Acres of Development Land	$ 800,000	$ 800,000	$ 800,000
Less: Cost of Sale		$ 32,000	$ 32,000
Adjusted Sales price		$ 768,000	$ 768,000
Less: Tax Basis		$ 40,000	
Equals: Gain on Sale		$ 728,000	
Less: Capital Gains Tax (federal and state)		$ 218,400	
Net Amount at Work	$ 800,000	$ 549,000	$ 768,000
Annual Return From Asset Valued at $800,000 @ 3.5% (land continues appreciating at 6%) $ 28,000			
Annual Return From Asset Reinvested in Balanced Acct. @ 10%		$ 54,960	
Avg. Annual Return From Asset in 6% CRUT reinvested @ 10%			$ 88,189
After-Tax (31%) Spendable Income	$ 19,320	$ 37,922	$ 60,850
Statistical Number of Years for Cash Flow for Joint Lives	31	31	31
Taxes Saved from $210,016 Deduction at 31% Marginal Rate			$ 65,105
Tax Savings and Cash Flow over Joint Life Expectancies	$ 598,920	$1,175,594	$1,951,461
Total Increase in Net Cash Flow Compared to Original Asset		$ 576,674	$1,352,541
Value of Assets After Estate Tax (at 55%) Paid	$2,678,764	$ 302,280	$ 0
Value of Charitable Remainder to Family Sponsored Charity			$2,590,566
Optional Use of Wealth Replacement Trust (WRT) to Offset Gift**			$3,968,815
Total Value to Family (Income and Heirs' Inheritance)***			$5,144,409

CHAPTER 6

ANNUITY TRAPS
AND TAX DISASTERS:
AN ANNUITANT'S SURVIVAL GUIDE

One of the "last" pure tax shelters is a personally-owned commercial annuity policy.[1] Straightforward as they may be, these products are creatures of some of the most complicated tax law you'll ever want to know.

Let's start by giving an overview of why they're so popular today.[2] Then I'll describe 20 or more financial traps and tax minefields that await an unwary policyholder. Whether you own annuities now or are considering a purchase, this is information you must know. You'll learn how fascinating

---

1 I'll discuss *Commercial* annuities in this chapter. They are sold by insurance companies that issue a contract to the *owner* of the annuity. *Private* annuities are transactions between individuals where one party sells a capital asset to a second party who usually makes payments for the lifetime of the first party. *Charitable gift* annuities are arrangements between individuals and charities that provide cash flow and tax deductions for contributors.

2 See Judith Burns, "Annuities becoming better buy, study says," Dow Jones News Service, *Denver Post*, March 27, 1997, p. 10B, and Kara Fitzsimmons, "Retirees go for annuities in a big way," Dow Jones News Service, *Rocky Mountain News*, Aug. 27, 1997, p. 6B.

annuities are; you'll also discover how to avoid surprises and make wise decisions about managing your policy. Since there is precious little information on this subject for non-experts, I've made a special effort to give you all the up-to-date information available.

There are numerous reasons why annuities are a popular place to park money.[3] Let's briefly review some of them in the next few pages. (The first 11 reasons apply to both fixed and variable policies; while the remaining four pertain only to fixed annuities.) In many ways annuities may actually make the "ideal" investment plan.

BENEFITS OF FIXED AND VARIABLE POLICIES

Benefit 1: The insurer behind an annuity offers professional management of the client's funds.

Benefit 2: There aren't any income taxes as interest is accumulating in the policy. Let's say you place $100,000 in an annuity policy that earns 8 percent interest annually over a long period of time. Untouched, the policy is worth $1 million in 30 years, and you'll be an annuity "millionaire" at that time. (If your investment style is to pay taxes on say an 8 percent interest each year at a 40 percent rate, there is less than $400,000 at the end of a 40 year period.)

Even though there will eventually be taxes to pay, here's how tax-deferral really works to your advantage. At the end

---

3 You'll find a 1997 Gallup Survey for the Committee of Annuity Insurers interesting. It is available free on the Internet at http://www.Annuity-Insurers.Org.

of 30 years, imagine that you surrender the annuity policy and pay 40 percent taxes on the profit of $900,000 ($1 million less $100,000). After paying $360,000 in taxes, there is a net of $640,000. That's still $240,000 (60 percent) more than the $400,000 you'd have on the investment plan where taxes are paid each year.

Benefit 3: Advocates point out that tax-deferred build-up in annuities helps keep Social Security benefits tax-free.[4] (This occurs because the untaxed accumulation doesn't count as "provisional income" when it comes to taxing Social Security payments.)

Benefit 4: Since in about two-thirds of the states cash values and proceeds are partly if not fully protected from creditors, annuity values may just be the best way to build a "bulletproof" arrangement for retirement.

Benefit 5: An annuity policy saves death costs because policy values normally pass to a beneficiary outside the process of probate.

Benefit 6: Annuities come with a free-look, free-return, no obligation period provided by state law or administrative ruling. Consequently, wherever a policy is purchased there is, for example, a 10-20 day cooling off period that begins after the policy is accepted.

Benefit 7: Some annuities offer Nursing Home Waiver of surrender charges, and benefits in the event of a terminal illness.

---

4 If your "provisional income" (adjusted gross income on your tax return plus tax-exempt interest from municipals plus half of Social Security income) exceeds a certain amount, expect to pay a hefty income tax on your Social Security payments.

Benefit 8: You can exchange one annuity policy for another tax-free under the Internal Revenue Code.

Benefit 9: Annuities are used as a vehicle to legally avoid a suspension in Medicaid benefits if someone enters a nursing home.

Benefit 10: There is even a new breed of annuity that can provide stock market like returns, without the risk. These products are called Equity Indexed Annuities, and they offer upside opportunity (usually based on the Standard and Poor's market index), and a guaranteed rate floor of around three percent, too.

Benefit 11: Finally, all annuities provide an income that you (or your beneficiary) can't outlive. (In fact, a recent survey indicates that 49 percent of annuity investors chose these products because of their lifetime income features.[5]) Whether you "annuitize" a deferred annuity after its accumulation years or you purchase an immediate annuity with cash, the policy offers a long and continuous liquidation of your money with interest. You can't get this with any other investment.

Fixed annuities[6] have some special advantages listed below:

Benefit 12: There is no market risk.

---

5 See Kara Fitzsimmons, "Retirees go for annuities in a big way," Dow Jones News Service, *Denver Post*, Aug. 27, 1997, p. 6B.

6 Fixed annuities are designed for conservative investors who want safety, competitive interest and a guarantee of principal. *Variable* annuities offer flexibility and the investment options of a group of mutual funds. *Equity indexed* annuities combine a minimum guarantee–usually 2-3 percent with upside potential based on a stock market index-usually Standard & Poors.

Benefit 13: They are especially liquid; lenders usually accept them as 100 percent loan collateral.

Benefit 14: Most insurers pay good, set rates of return (usually comparable to U.S. Treasuries, and sometimes with bonus interest as well). They are safe, also, because Insurance Guaranty Funds in all states give coverage (typically $100,000 or more) if an insurer has financial difficulty; this can be valuable protection for a serious accumulation plan.[7]

Benefit 15: And, there is always a guaranteed minimum rate of interest–normally three or four percent.

The bottom line: There is always value in putting aside money that is certain to be there someday. In most cases, however, "a penny earned is a penny taxed," and it isn't very safe either. With an annuity the tax comes later, and if it is a fixed policy the cash is predictable too.

These are some of the reasons why annuities have become such a popular investment in recent years. In fact, sales in 1996 exceeded $100 billion–a new high in the insurance industry. Today, annuities are not only sold by insurance agents, but they are recommended regularly by stock brokers, financial planners, accountants, bankers, and even lawyers (for Medicaid planning and lawsuit settlements). You'll even find annuities promoted as an alternative to cash lottery and sweepstakes winnings.

There are a few problems with annuities, however, and

---

7 Since insurers must reserve over $1 for each dollar in an annuity policy, it's virtually impossible for a policyholder to lose money anyway. The safety record of annuity policies is impeccable, indeed.

most consumers aren't informed of the "downsides" of these products. For all the good news, some of the problems can be shocking and perhaps disastrous if you haven't planned for them in advance. There are even a few traps that salespersons are not aware of, and "experts" don't seem to understand fully. I'll describe about two dozen annuity pitfalls that await the uninformed. If some of this information seems complicated, I suggest reading it more than once–especially if you and family have put away some serious money in annuity policies.

MISTAKES TO AVOID WITH ANNUITIES

MISTAKE #1:

Misunderstandings regarding withdrawal or surrender charges. It is true that in most cases, there aren't any direct sales or administrative expenses when there is a deposit in an annuity policy. Consequently, all this money earns interest from the day a contract is acquired. Be aware, however, that there may be surrender charges or early withdrawal penalties to take out an early distribution. Consider this example:

You deposit $100,000 in an annuity policy earning eight percent interest that is credited perhaps at the end of each year. There are surrender charges that decline (say 9-8-7-6-5 percent) over a five year period. Fortunately, there is a feature that protects 10 percent of policy values each year from

DON'T FEEL SO BAD... WE GET LOTS OF PEOPLE DOWN HERE FOR EARLY WITHDRAWAL PENALTIES.

these charges if some money is withdrawn. Here's the math:

At the end of one year, the policy is worth $108,000 ($100,000 + interest of $8,000). You can obtain $10,800 (10 percent) without a withdrawal charge; but there is a tax on $8,000, the portion of this distribution that represents taxable interest. Now if you withdraw an extra $10,000 (above the 10 percent penalty-free limit), the insurer assesses a nine percent withdrawal charge of $900 on this amount. (Since you've already paid tax on the interest, this second payment is income tax-free, however.)

Instead of withdrawing $10,800 from this policy let's say you surrender the annuity contract at the end of the first year. Here's truly a tax minefield. The following sets up the financial picture:

Value of policy ($100,000 plus interest of $8,000	$108,000
Less: A 10 percent penalty-free payment	-10,800
Distribution subject to surrender charges	$ 97,200
Less: A 9 percent surrender charge on $97,200	- 8,748
	$ 88,452
Net distribution before taxes ($10,800 plus $88,452)	$ 99,252

Now for the tax story: Since there is less ($99,252) than your original premium ($100,000), you'd think there would be a tax loss? There isn't.

Tax Minefield #1: As a matter of fact, it appears under the law that surrender charges aren't tax deductible; if not, you'll receive a 1099 form that taxes interest of $8,000 earned for the year. (For instance, if your tax bracket is 40 percent, you'll owe $3,200.)

Tax Minefield #2: If you are under age 59 1/2 at time of surrender, there is a 10 percent excise tax on the full profit of $8,000 (before deducting a surrender charge) as well. This could amount to an extra $800 tax bill.

My recommendation: Don't cash-in a policy until surrender charges have expired unless possibly you can make a tax-free Section 1035 exchange into a new contract that gives a "built-in" bonus to offset any penalty charges in your present policy.

MISTAKE #2:

Not reading the "fine print." In addition to withdrawal charges, determine if an annuity has surprise charges, fees or financial "traps" that are buried in fine print. These can significantly affect the performance of a policy. Here's are examples:

· *Back end loads:* Even though withdrawal fees have expired, there may be an obscure fee at surrender of the policy, or at death of the owner when the policy is cashed-out. This charge is an incentive to annuitize, or take an income from the annuity contract, instead.[8] Sometimes, annuity sales-persons neglect to explain this feature. And the charges can really mount up—to as much as 10 percent of the final value of the policy. *My recommendation:* If an annuity policy has a high back-end fee, don't buy it!

•   *Surrender charges at death:* In your 70s or 80s, a new policy may also include a surrender charge on a cash-out at death of the annuitant. This is an incentive for a beneficiary to annuitize the policy as well. *My recommendation:* If you are in your 70s or 80s and purchase an annuity policy, con-sider naming a younger spouse or relative as the annuitant—especially if there are surrender charges when an annuitant dies.

•   *Incentive bonuses:* It's common for an insurer to offer an attractive first year extra interest rate. However, this "bo-nus" may not be available if the policy is surrendered later; it is usually added only if the contract is annuitized. (In other words, the bonus is taken away unless you use the policy eventually for annuity income.) A word of caution: With some policies, bonuses are optional and salespersons offer them as inducements to buy. Since a discretionary bonus may reduce commissions, some states have enacted laws to forbid these credits as a form of rebate. They also may be a discriminatory sales practice they tend to encourage placing more money in the policy.

---

8 For an in-depth explanation of alternative annuity income arrangements, you may find it helpful to read the chapter on Commercial Annuities in my book, *Preserving Family Wealth Using Tax Magic - Strategies Worth Millions!* (Berkley, 1995).

·   *Interest rate history:* As an incentive to purchase, insurers frequently give a high interest rate for the first year or two. Keep in mind, however, that the company can always reduce future rates to the minimum guarantee in the contract; say three or four percent.[9] By checking interest rate histories, you'll learn whether or not an insurer maintains a competitive position on in-force policies. Ask an agent for this information.

·   *"Interest bailout:"* Some policies allow a policyowner to withdraw funds from the policy without a surrender charge, if interest rates on renewal are decreased to a specified level. Be aware, however, that there is only a limited "window" (perhaps 10 days) to take action after receiving the insurer's notice of reduction. (Not all companies have a notification procedure in place). So if your annuity has an interest bailout feature, ask the company to provide in writing their notification procedure when interest rates change. Keep in mind, also, that a bailout provision increases the risk assumed by an insurer (and it should theoretically decrease the interest rate paid in the policy). If it doesn't, this may indicate the insurance company is undertaking an extra risk that it shouldn't assume.

·   *Market value adjustments:* Some annuities always guarantee principal. When interest is credited, principal is in-

---

9 See Susan Pulliam, "Miffed Annuity Holders Head for Court," *The Wall Street Journal,* Sept. 17, 1997. In August of 1996, an elderly Kentucky man sued an insurance company and claimed it used a high first year promotional interest rate to induce customers. Then, the insurer dropped its rate sharply. The insurer is defending this lawsuit vigorously.

creased and guaranteed thereafter. Other policies may have a market value adjustment during the life of the contract, or at least for a period when there are surrender charges. For instance, if economic interest rates increase, the market adjustment factor is less than 100 percent and principal is reduced. However, if rates have decreased, the factor is positive and you'll have more. Negative market adjustments can really be significant; you must check on them to avoid surprises in an annuity policy.

My recommendation: At the end of this chapter, I list 20 questions to ask before an annuity is purchased. If you are serious about getting the most value from an annuity premium, do your homework. Compare and contrast policies by the answers you receive. By the way, if your agent can't answer these questions, ask him or her to call someone in a home office and get the information.

MISTAKE # 3:

Withdrawing funds from an annuity policy before age 59 1/2. It seems that most annuities are purchased by older people who use them to park serious money for emergencies or a rainy day. But younger savers find annuities attractive as well; for the good reasons I've shown you. Unfortunately, Congress has imposed an insidious excise tax for the younger, unwary client –a 10 percent penalty tax on pre 59½ distributions of policy profit.

There are some exceptions to the pre 59½ excise tax, and here are a few of them. The tax isn't assessed if you are disabled, or if another annuitant dies and you are beneficiary of the policy. There is no penalty tax, either, if you take a series of payments over your life expectancy. *My recommendation*: Annuities are long-range savings programs. If you're under 59½, or your needs are short-term, put money in a savings account instead.

MISTAKE #4:

Owner, annuitant and annuity beneficiary–choosing the wrong combination. In addition to the insurer, there are three parties to each annuity; the owner of the policy, the annuitant and the beneficiary.

In most cases, owner and annuitant are the same person. An owner can change the beneficiary and makes all decisions regarding adding or withdrawing money prior to the annuitant's death. An annuitant is like the insured in an insurance policy; annuity policies continue until annuitants die (or reach a maximum age–say 85 or 90), or the policy is surrender or annuitized. The beneficiary has no voice in the policy, but he or she receives the proceeds when an annuitant dies. A word of caution: Some annuity policies pay annuity income to the annuitant; some pay benefits to the owner. Check your policy for the precise language.

Unfortunately, it's easy to make a mistake when a policy is acquired. Let's say Harry and his wife, Mary, take out an annuity policy and own it jointly. Harry is annuitant and a daughter, Janice, is beneficiary because they want her to have this money after their deaths.

When Harry dies, the policy is terminated. The mistake: Unfortunately, Janice "inherits" the money even though Mary is still alive. What's more, since Mary then owns the policy, she makes a taxable gift of the value of the policy to Janice indirectly. In other words, Mary is treated as cashing-out the policy; she'll pay income taxes on policy profit, and then she may owe gift taxes as well on the gifts to her daughter.

My recommendation: Mary should be the primary beneficiary; Janice can be contingent beneficiary. Alternatively, Harry could name Mary co-annuitant, and Janice the beneficiary. Each approach permits Mary to continue the policy until she dies when Janice takes everything eventually.

Here's another problem that frequently occurs when the parties aren't paying attention to ownership and annuitant designations.

Let's assume Harry (age 70) and Mary (age 65) Johnson acquire an annuity policy, he is the owner and annuitant, and the policy matures at his age 80. The problem: Income taxes are due in 10 years at the maturity date.

My recommendation: The Johnsons should name Mary as the annuitant. This gives them 15 instead of 10 years to accumulate tax-deferred interest in the policy. Keep in mind that if Harry dies first, his younger spouse can then use the step-into-the-deceased-spouse's-shoes rule in the law and elect to continue the policy as new owner. (See Mistake #15.)

MISTAKE # 5:

Setting up joint ownership with a child. As a means to pass property outside probate, a parent might purchase an annuity as joint owner with a child. When the parent dies, this policy then "belongs" to the son or daughter. Simple in concept, this can be a tax disaster.

Let's say Harry acquires a $100,000 annuity contract, and he includes son Marty as equal owner in joint tenancy with right of survivorship. First, Harry in effect makes a $50,000 taxable gift to Marty. Secondly, both owners must sign forms to modify, surrender or exchange the policy; and this complicates matters. Third, all withdrawal checks are paid jointly. Fourth, when interest is taken, each owner gets a 1099 form for one-half, and on distributions the other owner makes a gift to the "distributee." Fifth, since Harry contributes the entire premium, 100 percent of its value will be included in his estate tax base eventually. Finally, when it comes to Medicaid planning, be aware that placing any asset in joint ownership can trigger a "look-back" period and result in a period of ineligibility for benefits.

My recommendation: Do not name a child joint owner of your annuity policy. Instead, when a child is the annuitant, name him or her successor owner. Then, a child who survives your death becomes the new owner, outside of probate. Know also that the policy must be annuitized, or cashed-out within five years after you die.

Some policies do not permit successor ownership. If so, it's likely the owner's estate (or the beneficiary) becomes the successor owner. In a few cases, insurers permit two beneficiaries—one at the owner's death and one at the death of an annuitant; in others, at an owner's death the new owner may automatically be the annuitant. The important thing is to read the contract, and make sure you know what will happen.

MISTAKE # 6:

Naming a trustee policy owner and beneficiary. When a funded revocable living trust-RLT is being used for privacy or probate avoidance, it seems natural to make it the owner-beneficiary of an annuity policy (and other personal assets as well). This can potentially be a tax disaster, if you are married.

Let's say you name an RLT owner-beneficiary of a $100,000 annuity policy (that names you as annuitant); the trust provides benefits for your spouse at your death. Then, this RLT must pay an income tax at a current rate of 39.6 percent rate on most of the profit on the policy. If instead, you keep ownership, and a spouse is the beneficiary individually, he or she can continue the policy (and it's tax deferral, too).

My recommendations: If your objective is trust management for spouse and family, a trust beneficiary approach probably makes sense. If however the goal is income tax deferral, specify your spouse beneficiary of an annuity policy that names you the owner-annuitant. Then, he or she can "step-into your shoes" as owner (see Mistake #15) and continue the policy indefinitely, or at least until any maturity date specified in the contract is reached.

MISTAKE # 7:

Selecting a minor child as beneficiary. Sometimes an annuity owner names a minor child beneficiary of the policy. If there is a will that names a guardian for the minor's property, this may be an acceptable arrangement. However, there still can be repercussions, especially in the aftermath of a divorce.

The *trap*: When a minor inherits property from a parent, usually the surviving parent assumes custody of this property and the child. *My recommendation:* To prevent an ex-spouse custodial parent getting at the money, the beneficiary for a minor child should be a trust where a reliable person is in charge. Then, if an ex-spouse assumes custody of the child, a trust still controls the annuity benefits.

CAUTION: If there isn't a trust, don't name a guardian beneficiary as an individual beneficiary: This causes the cash to belong to this person without legal restrictions. Instead, name the minor child beneficiary: This way, a probate court will make sure the appointed guardian uses these funds to benefit your descendant. But again, it's always best to name a trust beneficiary for minor children, especially if your goal is to withhold funds from their direct control at age 18 when guardianships are usually terminated.

MISTAKE # 8:

Pledging an annuity policy as collateral for a loan. If you acquire a policy after Aug. 13, 1982 withdrawals of profit in the contract are taxable; tax law refers to this as LIFO (last in, first out) tax accounting. If you borrow from the policy or pledge it for a loan commitment, there is another tax trap: You pay taxes as if a taxable withdrawal was made directly from the policy. (Be aware: There may be a 10 percent excise tax also if the owner-borrower is not age 59 ½.) Let me explain:

In 1998, Harry purchases an annuity policy for $100,000, and after a few years there is $125,000 on hand. Naturally if he withdraws $30,000 (which consists of $25,000 profit and $5,000 from the original investment), he'll receive a 1099 form stating that $25,000 is taxable. But let's assume this loan is made at a bank by pledging a policy as collateral. The result: The full accumulated profit of $25,000 is still included as income on his tax return.

The solution: If an annuity policy has surrender charges, it is probably better to pledge it instead of withdrawing the cash value. However, if you aren't yet ready to pay the income tax, obtain cash from other sources instead of pledging the annuity policy in a loan transaction.

My recommendation: If you have an annuity that is a pre-Aug. 14, 1982 policy, consider withdrawing annuity values or pledging this policy to your lender. The funds you receive are taxed on a FIFO (first in, first out) basis. On these contracts, there is no income tax (or a 10 percent excise tax) until the original investment is removed from the contract.

MISTAKE # 9:

Gifting annuity policies that have profit. When gifting an annuity policy (to family or charity) acquired after April 22, 1987, there is a tax minefield: The donor owes income tax on any profit in the policy unless the donee is your spouse. (Be aware: There may also be a 10 percent excise tax also if you are not age 59 ½).

Let's assume that on Jan. 1, 1995, you acquire a policy with $100,000 and gift it to a child when it is worth

$125,000. Since the contract has a $25,000 profit, you pay income tax (and possibly gift taxes too) when this gift is made. However, there is one consolation. Your child's basis for future income taxes is increased to $125,000 once the gift is made. (If this policy was purchased before April 23, 1987, a donor waits until the donee surrenders the policy or receives taxable income from it; then the donor pays a tax on up to any profit at time of the gift. The donee pays tax on the remaining profit, if any.)

My recommendation: In selecting assets for gifting, give cash or capital assets such as securities or real estate (instead of annuities) if the objective is not to pay tax on any profit at time of the gift. Keep in mind, however, that if the donee eventually sells a capital asset, he or she then pays a capital gains tax on profit above the donor's basis.

MISTAKE # 10:

Gifting annuity policies to children jointly. If an annuity policy is transferred to several children in joint tenancy, know that all owners must sign to make changes in the future. Therefore, if one wants to withdraw some money, each must consent by signing the insurer's forms.

This can get complicated; in addition to income taxes due on the profit, there are several tax traps for the unwary. First, a gift of the policy may not qualify for $10,000 annual exclusions (if under state law all owners must act together to make changes). Second, if there are surrender charges each child should maintain records for his or her own purposes. Third, the insurer will likely issue 1099's to all three children even though only one child makes a withdrawal. Finally, it is possible that policyowners who don't withdraw are making a gift to those that do.

My recommendation: Do not gift annuity policies, especially when there is more than one donee. Other assets make better gifts, especially if they aren't placed under the control of children in a joint form of ownership.

MISTAKE # 11:

Exchanging a deferred college annuity for an immediate annuity to "beat" the pre 59 1/2 10 percent penalty tax. Notwithstanding the 10 percent excise tax on premature distributions, it is common practice to purchase deferred annuities for college funding. The plan is that you will beat this penalty tax by converting (or exchanging) the policy into an immediate four or five year income annuity for tuition and other school expenses. Unfortunately, this can be a tax disaster. Here are the rules:

Let's suppose you acquire a deferred annuity (purchase date July 1, 1998) to fund a son's education. At say his age 18 in 2006, this policy is replaced by an immediate annuity contract that makes payments to him or her directly. The result: Under the law, if you are not age 59½ in 2006, a 10 percent excise tax is added to income taxes on the taxable portion of each payment.

The reason: To qualify under the excise tax exemption, payments from an immediate annuity must commence within one year of purchase. Under the law, the purchase date of this immediate annuity contract is deemed the date of the original policy; obviously, these payments began eight years (and not within one year) after that annuity contract was acquired. That's why the policy doesn't meet the excise tax definition of an immediate annuity.

My recommendation: Don't purchase a deferred annuity if you will be under age 59½ when payments are taken for your child's education. If you do, you owe a penalty–plus income tax on the profit portion of each distribution. Some good news: If an annuity is gifted to a custodian under the Uniform Gift to Minors Act, your minor child pays all of the taxes. Consequently, the overall rate may still be low (say 15 percent income tax plus the 10 percent penalty).

MISTAKE # 12:

Exchanging a policy issued before January 19, 1985, where the annuitant is a descendant of the owner. It used to be popular to acquire annuity policies where, for example, a grandchild is the annuitant. The notion was that there could be tax deferral for many, many years. What a great idea.

For instance, your grandson, Tommy, is age five. With $100,000, you purchase an annuity policy and name Tommy the annuitant. At your death, the policy belongs to Tommy and it is continued until he dies or annuitizes the contract. Voila! Everyone gets 70 or 80 years of tax deferral, over Tommy's life expectancy.

In 1985, Congress determined that this arrangement is tax abuse. Now, there is a tax trap. Newer policies (issued after Jan. 18, 1985) like these must be annuitized within one year after a holder (owner) dies–or cashed-in, instead, within five years of death. Consequently, when you die, Tommy is prohibited from continuing this policy for more than five years.

Here's the good news. There are some annuity policies (like Tommy's) still around that are pre-Jan. 19, 1985 contracts. These are "grandfathered" and may be continued until the annuitant dies. Now, for the bad news. If along the way one of these policies is exchanged for another contract, the new policy must follow the post-Jan. 18, 1985 rules. In other words, if Tommy's policy is replaced, the new one can't be maintained after the death of its owner. The government clearly wants the tax money sooner instead of later. *My recommendation:* Be careful when exchanging a pre-Jan. 19, 1985 annuity policy. It can be better to maintain the old contract as is if extended tax deferral may be important.

MISTAKE # 13:

Exchanging an annuity for a life insurance policy. It is possible, of course, to trade one annuity policy tax-free for another. You may even trade a life insurance policy tax-free for an annuity. But, you cannot exchange an annuity contract tax-free for a life insurance policy. Here's why:

The "profit" in a life insurance policy is usually income tax-free at death. For years, IRS has provided this "incentive" for taxpayers to insure their lives and protect their families. But when you exchange an annuity (that always costs someone income tax on its profit) for a life insurance policy that becomes tax-free at death, IRS draws the line.

The profit in the annuity policy is taxable when the exchange is made.

Example: Let's suppose you deposit $100,000 in an annuity policy that is now worth $250,000. These values are exchanged for say a $500,000 policy. The result: You owe income taxes on $150,000 ($250,000 less $100,000). My advice: To avoid taxes on your annuity profit, use other money to acquire the life insurance. As another option, annuitize the annuity and apply the annual payments to the new insurance policy. This way, you'll pay income tax evenly as the annuity profit is received over a period of time.

MISTAKE # 14:

Exchanging for an annuity policy without identical features. One of the advantages of annuity policies is the owner's ability to make a so-called 1035 tax-free exchange of one contract for another. If a new policy offers more than an old one, it's normal to trade the former for the latter. Consider this example:

Let's say in a period of declining rates, you own an annuity policy with Company A that has been paying nine percent interest for seven years. There are no surrender charges, and the rate is just lowered to five percent when other policies are paying seven percent. Although a new policy has some surrender charges, you decide to exchange policies. Here are the rules:

There is no tax on the exchange profit if (a) the annuitant (and preferably the owner and beneficiary) on each one are the same, (b) the entire policy is assigned to the new company —all of the money must be transferred, (c)all loans are repaid before the exchange, and (d) according to some—the retirement or maturity dates on both policies are identical. A fixed annuity can even be exchanged tax-free for a variable policy, or vice versa.

Here are a few examples of tax minefields that make the exchange taxable. Let's suppose you are the annuitant on Company A's policy, and your spouse becomes the annuitant on a new Company B contract (the annuitants aren't identical). Or you transfer merely a portion of the funds held in an existing policy (and the contract isn't assigned.) Or the maturity date with Company B is age 90 and the former company uses age 80.

Know also that the preferred way to exchange policies is to assign an old one to the new company. The second insurer then surrenders the policy and issues a new contract. If instead you cash-in the old policy, you may pay taxes even though the money is sent directly to a second company.

My recommendation: When making a 1035 exchange, always assign an old contract to the new carriers, and watch all paperwork closely during the trade-in process. Be aware, also, that the first company may issue a 1099 form (even though a 1035 exchange is completed property). If the form reports taxable income, ask the former insurer to send a statement (or a new form) indicating that the exchange is tax-free.

MISTAKE #15:

Not understanding the annuity distribution rules. One

of the least understood areas of tax law is what happens when an annuity owner or the annuitant dies. The IRS hasn't issued new rules for years, and it appears that even insurance companies are confused about how to report profit in the policy as taxable income. To help you better understand the possibilities, I recommend that you use these pointers if you and your family are parties to an annuity policy.

1.   If you are married, name one spouse owner and annuitant; the other spouse should be beneficiary. If the owner-annuitant dies, the beneficiary has 60 days to notify the insurer of a desire to step-into-the shoes of the deceased spouse-owner (and maintain tax deferral within the contract), or choose an income instead. A word of caution: If the beneficiary is also the owner, there is no step-into-the-owner's shoes option; he or she has merely 60 days to annuitize, instead, or pay income taxes on profit in the contract.

2.   If your policy was acquired after Jan. 18, 1985, and a child is annuitant, it matures if you die before your child. Be aware that the beneficiary then has only 60 days after a lump sum becomes available to annuitize. Otherwise, he or she pays income taxes on any profit in the contract.

My recommendation: To avoid tax surprises for your family, always get good advice when it comes to all decisions regarding owner, annuitant and beneficiary.

If you want to give your advisors more information about these and other complicated annuity matters, ask them to order *The Annuity Blue Book: How To Avoid Hidden Traps and Tax Disasters When Selling Annuities* by Richard W. Duff and Tyrone Clark. They should contact RWD Enterprises, P.O. Box 102244, Denver, CO 80210-2244, or at http://www.mcomm.com/duff to obtain a copy.

MISTAKE # 16:

Assuming the profit in an annuity policy is tax-free at death. Most investments provide a basis step-up when the owner dies. For example, the IRS "forgives" capital gains taxes on bonds, stocks or real estate that you own at death. The trap: This isn't true for fixed annuity policies or pensions, royalties or deferred salary arrangement(s) where profit at death becomes untaxed ordinary income. (There is a basis step-up for variable annuities, however, but only if the policy was issued before Oct. 21, 1979.)

Let's take an example where an annuity premium was $100,000. At the annuitant's death, the policy is worth $300,000 and there is a "profit" of $200,000. On receipt, heirs owe income taxes on everything over the original deposit of $100,000. They may also owe an estate tax on $300,000; if so, there is probably an income tax deduction for part of the estate tax paid.

My recommendation: Annuitize the annuity policy before death, and pay taxes gradually on profit until you die or payments stop. You gift the annuity payments to children who acquire a policy that insures your life. The financial results can be intriguing.

MISTAKE # 17:

Bequeathing profit annuity policies to a $600,000 "ex-

emption" trust. You have done some comprehensive estate planning, and your will leaves $600,000 to an "exemption" trust. The balance of your assets pass tax-free, as well, to a spouse.

To make things "simple," let's say there is an annuity policy-original premium $100,000-current value $600,000, and its beneficiary is your "exemption" trust. Other assets worth $1 million will belong to your spouse.

The problem: After income taxes of $200,000 (at a 40 percent assumed rate) are paid on profit of $500,000, the annuity is really only "worth" $400,000 to the trust. But it uses up a full $600,000 "exemption." *My recommendation*: Leave this policy to your spouse, and pass other "tax paid" assets worth $600,000 to the exemption trust. This way, your spouse's taxable estate will be reduced at his or her death by income tax paid on the annuity profit. The "exemption" trust is worth a full $600,000 because it receives tax-paid assets instead of taxable profit (in an annuity contract).

MISTAKE # 18:

Owning an annuity and making a charitable bequest the wrong way. Does your will make a bequest of real estate, cash or securities to charity? If there is an annuity policy, this instead may make the ideal charitable gift.

Let's assume you have an annuity policy where the original premium is $100,000. It is worth $300,000 today. You have stocks ($100,000 basis) presently valued at $300,000, and your will bequeaths these securities to the hospital or university. Perhaps these transactions should be reversed.

Here's why:

The annuity policy incurs income taxes on $200,000 when the family surrenders the contract, but there is no income tax on the securities. They get a basis step-up. *My recommendation*: Change the approach–name a charity beneficiary of the annuity policy, and pass securities to your family. When the charity receives its $300,000, so do your heirs.

MISTAKE #19:

A misunderstanding of equity-indexed annuities (EIAs). Equity-indexed annuities (EIAs) were introduced in 1995, and they typically promise a minimum rate of interest plus stock market-like returns. Since fixed annuities offer guarantees and variable annuities virtually make no promises, it's natural if EIAs (that offer both guarantees and upside growth) may seem confusing.

Let's say you pay a single premium of $100,000 for an EIA contract. After 7 years, it guarantees a minimum of $110,690 (which is 3 percent interest compounded annually on $90,000 from the original deposit). This EIA also credits "upside" returns measured by The Standard & Poor's index. To some, this seems almost too good to be true. How can the insurance company do this?

Some observations: Insurers can offer EIAs because they purchase quality bonds with a portion of the premium. The remaining dollars are used to pay commissions, improve their profit, and acquire call options which they sell at a gain if the market goes higher. However, insurance companies usually "cap" the growth rate. An example is a top upside of 80 percent of a maximum 12.5 percent profit. Thus, if the S&P index increases by 20 percent, this EIA only credits 10 percent (80 percent x 12.5 = 10).

My recommendation: Before you purchase an EIA, get a clear picture of how growth is recognized in the policy. If the crediting method is unclear, you may be more interested in a variable policy where appreciation is virtually unlimited, or simply a fixed policy where the rates are fully guaranteed. Also, keep in mind that these underlying guarantees are the bedrock for all EIAs.

MISTAKE # 20:

Using annuities as a foolproof method of sidestepping Medicaid regulations. Medicaid laws now permit states to approve annuities that provide income for the community (at-home) spouse and these funds won't count as a resource to the family. Let me explain.

Harry is institutionalized, and the family applies for Medicaid welfare benefits. He and his wife are entitled to limited resources and income; for example, in 1997 Colorado permits Harry to have some exempt assets such as a home and auto, and a monthly income of $1,452. In addition, his wife can have $79,020 in non-countable resources. Let's say Harry has an additional cash sum of $200,000. The result: This family isn't financially destitute. Medicaid is a welfare program, and they clearly do not qualify for it's benefits.

The *annuity solution:* Annuity payments (made to a community spouse) aren't countable as a resource, or income which prohibits Medicaid benefits. *My recommendation:*

Check your state's law. In the above example, Harry may be permitted to take $200,000 and purchase a single premium annuity that pays an immediate income to his spouse. The result: Her cash flow is increased, and it doesn't prevent them from qualifying for Medicaid benefits for Harry.

CAUTION: Medicaid laws are strict, and it's easy to run afoul of the state rules or type of annuity in the first place. There are also issues when annuities are acquired soon before or after an applicant enters the nursing home. Therefore, it's essential to check with an elder law attorney before making any decisions regarding "Medicaid" annuity contracts.

Conclusion

Annuities are more popular than ever, and you should consider them. Remember that these products have creditor protection and other advantages besides tax deferral. However, there is a downside or two as well. Before you buy, just ask some questions like those at the end of this chapter.

20 QUESTIONS TO ASK
BEFORE AN ANNUITY IS PURCHASED

1.   Are there any up-front sales charges?

2.   Are there any administrative or annual fees?

3.   If on surrender, can I receive less than the initial premium?

4.   What are the surrender charges and how long do they last?

5.   Are surrender charges charged to principal or on principal and interest?

6.   Will surrender charges be waived for a partial withdrawal of, say, 10 percent annually?

7.   Can I take this partial withdrawal during the first year without a surrender charge? If so, how is everything calculated?

8.   Is there a "bail out" clause where surrender charges are waived if the initial interest rate decreases? If so, how much must the interest rate decrease?

9.   If the interest rate does decrease and the surrender charges are waived, how many days do I have to surrender before surrender charges reappear?

10. Will surrender charges be waived if the annuitant dies?

11. Will surrender charges be waived if the owner annuitizes? If so, what is the minimum annuitization period for these charges to be waived? (5 years certain? Or must this option have a life contingency?)

12. Unless already noted, in what other instances, if any,

are surrender charges waived?

13. Does the annuity policy describe how renewal rates will be declared? If so, how? If not, please describe this procedure.

14. What is the history of renewal rates for this specific annuity? What is the history of renewal rates for the insurance company's other annuities? How is the insurer rated by agencies such as Duff and Phelps, Standard and Poors, and Moody's?

15. For how long is the initial interest rate guaranteed; and is interest compounded daily, monthly or less frequently? (It makes a difference!)

16. Is there a market adjustment feature? If so, for how long and how is it calculated?

17. What are guaranteed settlement rates? Current settlement rates? (Use ages 65 and 75 and 10 years certain and life unless facts and circumstances indicate otherwise)

18. If the annuitant dies, will a death benefit be paid? If so, to whom (owner or beneficiary)?

19. If the owner dies, will a death benefit be paid? If so, to whom (annuitant or beneficiary)?

20. What other features, positive and negative, should I know?

CHAPTER 7

PERSONAL LIFE INSURANCE:
LIVING WITH IT
BECAUSE YOU CAN'T DIE
WITHOUT IT

I magine this scene in the early 1900s: A father calls his family together to announce how everyone must sacrifice because he has just acquired a $1,000 life insurance policy for their welfare.

Today, the average amount of life insurance per U.S. household is more than $120,000, and this figure is beginning to increase. I'm aware, however, that there isn't much of that "patriarchal" attitude left. Somehow, we seem to treat life insurance more casually than it deserves to be treated. It's as if we believe our increased life spans mean there will never be a death claim.[1]

I take life insurance arrangements seriously and believe coverage should be increased above $120,000 per household.

---

1 Sometimes even lawyers take life insurance lightly. At a speech before the American Society of Chartered Life Underwriters and Chartered Financial Consultants in October of 1997, Mike Thiessen, a partner in the Kansas City law firm of Husch & Eppenberger, remarked, "Many attorneys on my level in Kansas City don't believe in life insurance." But then he added—"and their firms' business is in decline." Sandy Hock, "Insurance Agent Must Estate His Case, " *Investment News,* Nov. 3, 1997, p. 13.

The following comments by John J. O'Connell say it all:

"Life insurance is a necessity and a responsibility, not a conversation piece. Perhaps you can make more money in the market. Some people do and some people do not. But, we are not talking about your making money in the stock market - we are concerned with a family spending money in the supermarket."[2]

It's up to each of us to make sure our life insurance program performs at peak level. We must manage our policies much like we handle a carefully selected portfolio of stocks, real estate and mutual funds. If we don't, the system certainly won't take care of it for us.

During the last 30 years, I've sold policies to people who were disabled the very next month, and even one who died the next day. I've even had people decline an offer for insurance, and, tragically, die weeks later. But, perhaps the most incredible life insurance story is attributed to Malcolm Forbes, former Chairman and Chief Stockholder of Forbes, Inc., who certainly squeezed the most out of a premium dollar.

In December 1989, *The Los Angeles Times* reported that much of the income of Forbes, Inc. was being used to purchase enormous sums of estate tax-free insurance.[3] Two months later, *The New York Times* stated that Steve Forbes

---

2 John J. O'Connell, L.L.M., J.D., *More Thoughts On Life And Life Insurance,* (LU Techniques, Jan., 1979.)

3 Michael Cieply, "The Wary Capitalist," *The Los Angeles Times,* Dec. 31, 1989, page D1.

(Malcolm's son) was in control of the company, to maintain his father's wish that Forbes, Inc. remain a family business.[4] One week later, *The New York Times* informed us that Malcolm had died.[5]

I'm told that Mr. Forbes was insured for well over $100 million, most of which was acquired within a year or two of his death. The important thing, however, is that he had the foresight to deal with his own mortality and take steps to perpetuate *Forbes* magazine for son, Steve, as well as the rest of us.

While most of us can't purchase millions of dollars worth of life insurance, we can make the most of the coverage we can afford. Read this chapter carefully to avoid getting into trouble, with those pesky life insurance policies we love to hate. Afterward, you should be able to improve your insurance program significantly.

AN OVERVIEW

When you acquire life insurance, it's important to view a relationship with the agent as a partnership which will continue for the life of the policy. The goals of this extended association are:

1.   Obtain a quality offer from the insurer;

2.   Avoid unnecessary income and taxes on the proceeds at death;

4 N.B. Kleinfield, "At Forbes, The Family Still Reigns," *The New York Times*, Feb. 27, 1990, page D1.

5 "Malcolm Forbes, "Lesson On Estate Taxes," *The Los Angeles Times*, March 4, 1990, page D1.

3. Adapt beneficiary designations to life's changing circumstances;

4. Shelter insurance proceeds from a surviving spouse's next mate;

5. Avoid losing control of cash values and benefits to creditors of the insured, policyowner and beneficiaries; and

6. Avoid losing insurance proceeds to someone's failed marriages.

During this relationship, an agent must help maintain protection during the best and worst of times - and with dispatch. It is your responsibility to organize everything and prepare for insurance checkups, at least annually, to discuss matters that are important to you.

LIFE INSURANCE TRAPS, MISTAKES AND TAX DISASTERS

ERROR #1:

An Inadequate Face Amount. Do you ever wonder whether your premium dollars acquire the optimum mix of face amount and cash value? Are you "top-heavy" on either death benefits or living cash buildup?

A few years ago, a California lawsuit was settled where a $50,000 "4-pay" annual premium acquired a $1 million policy owned by an insurance trust.[6] The insured died six months after this policy was issued, and (with considerable

---

6 See Mark T. Donohue, "Unexpected Liability Awaits Many Trustees of Life Insurance Trusts, " *Trusts and Estates Magazine*, April, 1994, p. 43 — an excellent article indeed.

hindsight) the beneficiaries sued the agent and trustee.

The lawyer argued, "The same $50,000 could have acquired a $2 million contract with the same company." This policy certainly would have provided much more bang-for-the-buck to the family at the insured's death. Unfortunately, we'll never know whether the agent and insured discussed this matter because the insured, of course, is dead, and the lawsuit was settled out of court.

I'm not suggesting that lawsuits are the answer whenever something goes wrong with your insurance policy. I am, however, recommending that you and your agent take a hard look at everything - at least annually. Be honest about your situation and pocketbook. Then, leave notes in a file that give family insights to decisions made about your insurance and financial requirements.

ERROR #2:

Not "Binding" The Policy. Once an application is signed, *always* pay a premium (if permitted by the insurer) for at least a month or two. The agent issues a conditional receipt confirming that under certain circumstances, you are insured.

For instance, this receipt may say that you are covered after a medical examination is taken. Or, there may be a statement that you are insured temporarily depending on how you answer three or four preliminary questions. Without this receipt, an insurer won't make an offer if your health changes for the worse before a policy is approved. With the receipt, you are usually protected and covered based on present medical and financial circumstances.

If you are not approved at standard rates, an insurer always refunds money on request. Since all states have a free-look period of usually an extra 10-30 days after you receive the policy, you even have some additional time to refuse an offer. Consequently, there is nothing to lose by binding the contract when an application is signed; there is always a money-back guarantee until at least the free-look term expires.

My recommendation: If allowed by the insurer, go ahead and bind the insurance. (Keep in mind that conditional receipts vary from company to company - always ask for an explanation. If the face amount exceeds binding limits, ask how at least a portion of the face amount can be bound.) If you don't bind the insurance, at least make a premium deposit the moment coverage is approved. You'll then have a free-look period that begins on the date of policy delivery. If everything isn't just right, you can ask for a refund.

ERROR #3:

Not Adding Waiver Of Premium (W/P). If you qualify (based on age and health), consider adding W/P to your policy. With this feature, the insurance company pays your premiums once you are disabled for a period of time – usually 90 or 180 days. The insurer also credits dividends and increases of cash value in the meantime. If your agent doesn't include W/P in the premium quotation, ask what it costs and whether you are eligible for it.

ERROR #4:

Mismanaging Premium Payments. Life insurance actuaries compute annual premiums and assume you'll pay them at the beginning of each year. If you pay more frequently (semiannually, quarterly or monthly), there is an extra "use of money" factor charged by the company, which can be expensive.

Instead of paying $10,000 annually, you may pay $5,400 semiannually, or $10,800 each year - an extra $800, or an 8 percent cost. Since you can only invest $5,000 for six extra months, the cost is nearly double or 16 percent, and it isn't tax deductible. Monthly premiums of $900-$10,800 each year would actually cost less because you'd have the "use of" some remaining portion of $5,000 over the course of each six-month period.

My recommendation: Ask an insurance agent to compare costs of annual, semiannual, quarterly or monthly premium payment alternatives. Normally, you'll find that annual or automatic monthly withholding is least expensive.

CAUTION: If you own term life insurance with no cash value, a missed premium can result in canceled coverage. All insurance policies provide a 30-day premium grace period, where there is still coverage, even with a missed payment. Most companies have an extra ten days grace or more, where you aren't covered but can still submit premiums without new health questions. After all grace periods, the coverage is canceled automatically, and a special procedure is necessary to reinstate a policy. Although insurers are usually lenient, there is no assurance that lapsed coverage will be returned as it was.

By using automatic withholding, it's likely that an agent will be notified if a premium check bounces. This amounts to a cross-check, where the agent can call you promptly if the policy is in danger of lapse.

I also recommend that you have some form of permanent coverage (universal, variable or whole life) instead of term insurance. Here, there are cash values that can be used to pay missed premiums automatically if you wish. Most importantly, keep insurance policies under control! It's one thing to voluntarily cancel coverage; it's quite another to lose a policy by inadvertently missing a premium payment.

ERROR #5:

The Wrong Policyowner. There was a time when $1 million of insurance was almost unimaginable. Today, it's likely that your next policy will be for at least $500,000, and perhaps $1 million or more.

Since a large policy can easily push an estate tax base over $600,000, an irrevocable trust (ILIT) should usually be named as the policyowner of a personal policy. An attorney prepares the trust document, and true: This can be costly. Unfortunately, this expense causes many insureds to forego a trust approach, using individual owner and beneficiary designations instead. It's important, therefore, to understand these ownership traps whenever you sign an application as the insured:

Traps Related to Naming the Policyholder:

Trap #1: Your Spouse is the Owner. Before 1982, when there was a 50 percent marital deduction (MD), it was popular for your spouse to own an insurance policy. If an insured died first, the proceeds were estate tax-free until the beneficiary passed away. Nowadays, this strategy is less important because most couples use an unlimited MD approach that "zeroes-out" taxes at the first death anyway.

Let's suppose your wife, Mary, owns a large policy insuring your life. Since there is no estate tax advantage, she transfers it to an ILIT that names her trust beneficiary. *The trap:* Since Mary keeps a lifetime interest in this trust, death proceeds are still part of her estate tax base.

If, instead, she gifts the policy to you, and you create the ILIT for her benefit, insurance proceeds remaining at her death should pass without any estate tax. If you use this approach, however, most advisors suggest there be some delay between these transfers. Otherwise, it will appear that she (instead of you) transferred the policy to her own ILIT. Also, be aware that there is a three-year "bring back" law whenever an insured gifts insurance to another party (see Chapter 9, Mistake #4). In other words, the proceeds are added to your estate tax base if you die within this three-year policy transfer period.

My recommendation: If estate tax avoidance is your goal, it's best to create an ILIT and name the trustee policyowner when you apply for a policy.

Trap #2: Your Children are the Owners. If an ILIT

doesn't seem appropriate, an adult child may be the next choice. The problem is that someday, he or she may be party to a divorce, lawsuit or family breakup. Under these circumstances, this policy can be lost to an unfriendly person just when the family needs it most. In addition, when children own a policy jointly, they cannot select one to be in control. An insurer will require that all owners agree before a policy change or right is exercised.

My recommendation: (a) Don't make children joint owners of a policy. Instead, obtain policies for each child individually; or (b) have children form a partnership or trust where a manager controls a single policy; or (c) best yet: You create an irrevocable trust where your spouse or one or more of your children are trustees and they can own the policy. A trust is more complicated but more flexible, and a creative lawyer can protect the trust insurance money from lawsuits, taxes and family conflict.

CAUTION: When creating the ILIT, do not name yourself trustee - this adds the insurance proceeds to your estate tax base.

Trap #3: There is No Successor Owner.. Let's say your son, Bill, owns your policy. It's important to also name a second owner if Bill passes away before you do. Without a successor, the policy passes through probate and belongs to his creditors, spouse, children, or possibly a former spouse if you are divorced.

My recommendation: When an individual owns your policy, always name a successor owner, just in case. Keep in mind, however, that any policyowner can choose a successor owner. If this concerns you, then place the policy in an irrevocable trust initially.

Trap #4: You Have an ABC Three-Cornered Policy. There is a special trap waiting to ensnare many policies presently in force. Let's say your wife, Mary, owns a policy that insures you. She names your son, Bill, beneficiary. Since Mary makes this decision, the law considers her to be making a gift of the insurance proceeds when you die, and she may then owe gift taxes as well. It's as if she receives the cash, and then gifts it to Bill.

This so-called "ABC three-cornered arrangement" often occurs when parents own policies that insure children, and grandchildren are the beneficiaries. *My recommendation:* Always make the owner and the beneficiary the same person. Then, on receipt of the proceeds, he or she can make $10,000 tax-free annual gifts to family members at leisure. This avoids a possible tax trap at death.

ERROR # 6:

The Wrong Beneficiary. Sometimes, it's difficult to select a primary or contingent beneficiary, and it seems acceptable temporarily to name your estate as recipient of the proceeds. But, if this isn't changed later, it can turn into a disaster at your death. Here's why:

When an estate is named beneficiary of an insurance policy, the proceeds are usually obtainable by estate creditors (and creditors of heirs, as well) to pay debts and administration expenses. Just imagine insurance cash that is the only asset on a list of probatable property, and all of this is unnecessarily lost to some crafty estate creditor.

My recommendation: Check policies for a beneficiary designation in favor of your estate. Then remove it and name individuals - or preferably a trust - as recipient of the insurance cash.

Traps Related to Naming the Beneficiary:

When an individual is named beneficiary, problems can arise that will make you wish you'd never obtained the insurance in the first place. Here's a list of potential beneficiaries where there could be problems:

Trap #1: A Surviving Spouse. When you name your spouse beneficiary, this may unnecessarily "push" his or her estate over $600,000. If a trust is named instead, it can be a "family trust" for your spouse's benefit only - while he or she is still alive. Then, it passes to children estate tax-free at your spouse's death.

When you leave insurance money directly to your spouse, it also becomes available to his or her new spouse, and cash is always tempting to a prospective suitor who wants to share in a windfall received at your death.

I remember a situation where an insured client was murdered while moonlighting as a cab driver. When his 25-year old widow collected a $1 million insurance benefit, she already had a boyfriend "advising" her on money matters. And this is real life, not fiction!

My recommendation: If these possibilities concern you,

create a trust for your spouse, and name the trust as beneficiary of your life insurance.

Trap # 2: A Former Spouse. If you are divorced, you'll probably chuckle at a situation I encountered a few months ago. After a divorce, a client changed his will in favor of his parents. When the client died unexpectedly, a $500,000 insurance policy was still payable to his former spouse. Due to his divorce, his parents questioned this. But, courts don't invalidate beneficiary designations in the case of a failed marriage.

My recommendation: When there is a marital breakup or when one is anticipated, and it isn't your intention to benefit a former marital partner, change all spousal beneficiary designations.

Trap # 3: Surviving Children In Equal Shares. In most states, a beneficiary designation in favor of "surviving children" probably includes illegitimate children as well. If you want to include only children of a lawful marriage, then designate "lawful surviving children" as the recipients.

Moreover, even when "lawful surviving children" are beneficiaries, the inevitable question is: "Who receives a child's share if he or she predeceases you?" Of course, the remaining children simply take more.

For example, your children: Bill, Judy, Ted and Carol are equal beneficiaries of a $600,000 policy. At your death, if only Bill and Carol are alive, they each receive $300,000. If either Ted or Judy have children (your grandchildren), they receive nothing.

If you want a group of grandchildren to receive a deceased child's share, specify as beneficiaries, "lawful surviving children per stirpes." If you want your daughter-in-law or son-in-law to participate as well, select a trust as beneficiary, and spell out your wishes in the trust agreement. A trust that includes a deceased beneficiary's spouse is also a permissible recipient of income and principal.

My recommendation: Consider all of the possibilities that can occur. If an agent doesn't have the correct language, call the insurance company. Although they won't give legal advice, their law departments will provide some alternatives that may solve the problem.

Trap # 4: Grandchildren, Where There is a Generation-Skipping Tax Due When You Set Aside Something For Them. Let's suppose you have already provided for children. Now, it's time to do something for the grandchildren. You acquire a $1 million policy ($50,000 annual premium), payable to five grandchildren, in equal shares - and you own the policy.

The problem is that at your death, there's a generation-skipping (GS) tax to pay on this transfer. Assuming the $1 million policy pays its own estate tax of $500,000 (at a 50 percent rate), there is an extra 55 percent GS tax of $177,420 ($500,000 ÷ 2.8182, a factor to use when the transfer bears its own GS tax as well). Although a portion of your $1 million GST exemption (if available) may avoid this GS tax when you die, it's just not best to name grandchildren beneficiaries of this policy.

My recommendation: Create a *vested trust* for grandchildren that owns your policy while you are alive. The goal is to shelter the insurance proceeds from GS tax and estate tax at your death. If the trust arrangement is carefully crafted, it accomplishes this, and there is also no need to allocate any portion of the $1 million GS exemption to your premium gifts.

CAUTION: Do not name grandchildren or more remote descendants as direct beneficiaries of your life insurance. With an attorney's help, create a vested trust for this arrangement instead.

Trap # 5: A Minor. When insurance proceeds become payable to a minor, his or her legal guardian manages the money until the recipient reaches adulthood under state law.

Let's say you're divorced, and you name children or grandchildren as beneficiaries. If they are still minors, it's possible that an in-law or former in-law will control the funds for many years! If you don't want this, pay the proceeds to a trust that's managed by someone friendly to your side of the family.

Trap #6: A Relative (Fiduciary). Let's assume that you have (or intend to have) a trust arrangement for your children. Your sister, Joyce, is named a direct recipient of an insurance policy, and the intention is that she will use the proceeds to benefit the children. But, titles like "trustee" or "guardian" aren't listed beside her name on the beneficiary designation form.

The result: It's likely that Joyce will receive this insurance money as her personal funds, without any legal obligation to benefit your children according to the plan. *My recommendation:* Specify in the trust instrument that Joyce is trustee. Then, designate as beneficiary of the policy, "Trustee Under Trust Agreement of the Insured dated _____." This way, she'll be obligated as a fiduciary to use the proceeds as you intend.

Trap #7: Your Spouse When He or She Isn't A U.S. Citizen. If your spouse isn't a U.S. citizen, you shouldn't name him or her beneficiary of your life insurance. Unfortunately, even though your spouse may be a permanent U.S. resident, there's no protection under the law for the unlimited marital deduction.

My recommendation: Consult a tax lawyer, and carefully explain your situation. Then, consider a qualified domestic trust (QDOT) for your beneficiary designation. Although there are some limitations, QDOT's qualify for a marital deduction and protect insurance from estate taxes.

Trap #8: There Is No Contingent Beneficiary. Without a named primary beneficiary living at the time of your death, the policy's proceeds are always payable to your estate. This could require probate, when there would otherwise be none.

For example, your son, Bill, is named beneficiary, but he predeceases you. Unless there is a new beneficiary, the proceeds are payable to your estate. *My recommendation:* Name a second (or even a third) individual or trust as beneficiary who receives the proceeds when Bill fails to survive you. Better yet: Create a trust arrangement for everyone that spells out all possible scenarios.

TRANSFERRING AND EXCHANGING POLICIES INCORRECTLY

A comprehensive wealth preservation plan usually suggests that an insured transfer his or her policies to others in the family. Here's what can go wrong:

MISTAKE #1:

A Gift To Children In Joint Tenancy. Let's suppose you gift a policy to three children in joint tenancy with right of survivorship. The contract has cash value of $50,000, and you assume that this gift fits within two annual gift tax exclusions of $60,000 (3 donees x $10,000 x 2 donors). However, in most states, these children must act collectively to make any policyowner changes. Consequently, this $50,000 cash value transfer will probably be treated as a future interest gift that doesn't qualify for $10,000 annual exclusions under the gift tax law.

The result: The transfer is a taxable gift. *My recommendation:* Name these children owners as tenants-in-common. Under the laws of their states, if they then can separate their rights individually, gifts to them will qualify for $10,000 annual gift tax exclusions under the Tax Code. Keep in mind, however, that the share of a tenant-in-common can pass by will, and a creditor of the estate or even a stranger may become an "owner-partner" sometime in the future.

MISTAKE # 2:

A Transfer With A Policy Loan. When gifting a policy with significant cash values, the natural tendency is to borrow this money before making the transfer. The loan reduces your taxable gift, if any. Besides, you might want the use of this money before you give up the policy permanently.

The problem is that when there's a loan that exceeds premium cost basis, a gift of the policy causes most of the proceeds (face amount less basis) to be taxable income when the insured dies.

For example, you have a $500,000 policy with cash values of $100,000 and plan to gift this policy to your daughter. The base premiums to date are $90,000. If, when the gift is made, you've borrowed more than $90,000 from the policy, you'll owe income tax on the profit and your daughter will have to pay an income tax at your death.[7]

My recommendation: Before transferring an insurance policy, make sure policy loans are limited to the premium cost basis — and not one penny more!

MISTAKE # 3:

A "Surprise" Gift Tax When You Transfer A Life Insurance Policy. When a policy is transferred, the insurer provides the gift tax value which is roughly the cash value at that time. What if, however, you are then unhealthy and perhaps uninsurable? Will the IRS say the gift tax value is nearer to the actual face amount of the policy?

---

7 See also Chapter 9, *Irrevocable Life Insurance Trusts, Mistake #13.*

If you transfer a policy under these circumstances, it may be necessary to establish what the real gift tax value of the policy is at that time. To determine this, ask a viatical settlement firm what they would pay for the contract under facts and circumstances that exist at the time.

MISTAKE #4:

An Improper Policy Exchange. It's possible to complete a tax-free exchange of a life insurance policy (prior to maturity) for an annuity or another life insurance contract. But a mistake can spell a tax disaster.

Let's say you've paid insurance premiums of $50,000, and the cash value is $70,000. Obviously, if this policy is surrendered, you pay income tax on $20,000. But, if this policy is exchanged for one issued by the insurer, or if it's assigned to a new insurer who makes the exchange and issues a new policy, there is no tax to pay.

CAUTION: If you and your spouse trade separate policies in exchange for one joint life policy, the IRS says this isn't a tax-free exchange. You won't have a tax-free trade either, if you surrender one policy and then purchase another. If you want everything tax-free, always assign a policy to a new insurer and let it make the exchange. Also, if a policy is exchanged with a loan (and the new policy cancels this loan), you'll pay income tax if the previous loan represents profit in the transaction. Let's say premiums on an old policy are $4,000, the cash value is $5,000 and the loan is $2,000 (the net cash is $3,000). If this loan is canceled in a tax-free exchange, you'll still owe tax on $1,000 - the profit in the policy.

My recommendation: To replace one insurance policy with an annuity or new life policy, ask the agent to use an assignment-exchange approach to protect your income tax position. These arrangements are particularly useful if there is a "loss" (the premium exceeds policy values) in the present policy. You'll still carry forward into the new policy the premium cost basis of the older policy!

MISTAKE # 5:

An Exchange or Transfer Of A Policy To A Foreign Person. Under the Taxpayer Relief Act of 1997, a tax-free exchange of a life insurance policy will, in effect, become taxable, if this has the effect of transferring a policy to a foreign person. The law is unclear on the definition of "transferring to a foreign person," so if this could affect you, I recommend checking with a tax advisor for more information.

MISTAKE # 6:

Surrendering A Policy With A Loan Against It. Life insurance policies are truly tax-favored products — as long as you keep them. As cash increases in the policy, there is no income tax. There is also no income tax on loans that exceed premiums. There isn't even income tax on any profit at death. But, there may be some tax surprises when you surrender a policy during your lifetime.

Let's suppose you've paid premiums of $22,000 (including $2,000 for double indemnity, waiver of premium and disability income benefits). The cash value is $25,000, and there is a policy loan of $25,000. You've only received $20,000 cash, however, because $5,000 in interest over the years has been added to an actual loan of $20,000. How much will be taxable income on a form 1099 provided by your insurer?

The answer is $5,000. Here's the math: Your premium cost basis is only $20,000 because the $2,000 for extra policy features isn't included. And you'll be taxed on the full profit of $5,000 ($25,000 cash value less a $20,000 basis), as if your borrowed amount is received at surrender and used to pay off the loan. Unfortunately, the loan interest of $5,000 isn't subtracted from the taxable income in the contract.

My recommendation: Don't be surprised by 1099s that tax you on "phantom income." Check with your insurer before you surrender the policy. It may make more sense to keep it.

It seems that life insurance policies are both a blessing and a curse. They provide huge amounts of tax-free cash for beneficiaries just at the right time. However, they can provide disappointments for insureds and beneficiaries if benefits are unnecessarily made subject to taxes, lawsuits and family conflict.

Since the rules don't always make common sense, it's best to check before you make changes in your policies or surrender them. Then, develop a relationship with a quality insurance agent who wants to help; your extra effort will pay dividends many times over.

CHAPTER 8

ESTATE DISTRIBUTION DOCUMENTS:

MAKE THEM SAY WHAT YOU MEAN AND MEAN WHAT YOU SAY

In general, a U.S. citizen can bequeath property as he or she sees fit.[1] Unfortunately, most people still die without a will that outlines who gets what, and when. It strikes me as ironic that someone can expend so much effort building their estate, yet drop the ball when it comes to preserving that wealth for their loved ones. Of course, there are others who make full use of the will as a final act of self-expression, rather than just a financial document. Consider the celebrated jazz pianist "Fats" Waller, who left only a dollar to his wife "for reasons known to her."[2] J. Paul Getty

---

1 This right is not absolute. In some states-(a) certain bequests to charities are invalid, (b) bequests to murderers are not upheld, (c) bequests against public policy aren't permitted, and (d) surviving spouses always have a right to elect against a will nonetheless.

2 Ultimately, a dower right established by law provided her with a third of the estate.

made special changes to indicate his disapproval of his children. In one codicil, for instance, he took away his youngest son's right to share in his father's wealth, and left him only $500. Twelve years later, however, Getty designated this son as an executor and trustee of the will with another brother, evidence that he was once again in his father's good graces.[3]

John (Jack) B. Kelly, Jr., father of Princess Grace of Monaco, concluded his will by telling his family that if he had to choose between leaving them worldly gifts or character, "I would give you character. The reason I say that, is with character, you will get worldly goods because character is loyalty, honesty, ability, sportsmanship and, I hope, a good sense of humor."[4]

In this chapter, we'll look at the consequences of a careless attitude toward one's will. This includes dying without a will, with a poorly written will, or even having a good one that doesn't do the best job. I'll also explain how revocable living trusts (RLTs), properly used, can help you accomplish the aims you set forth in your will. (See Illustration #1 for a full diagram of some usual estate and financial paperwork.) You'll learn strategies you can share with your lawyer, so that the wills and trusts you develop together won't create problems for your family.

---

3 Gordon W. Brown, *Administration of Trusts and Estates* (Lawyer's Cooperative Publishing and Del Mar Publishing, 1993), p. 83.

4 Brown, *Administration of Trusts and Estates*, p. 69.

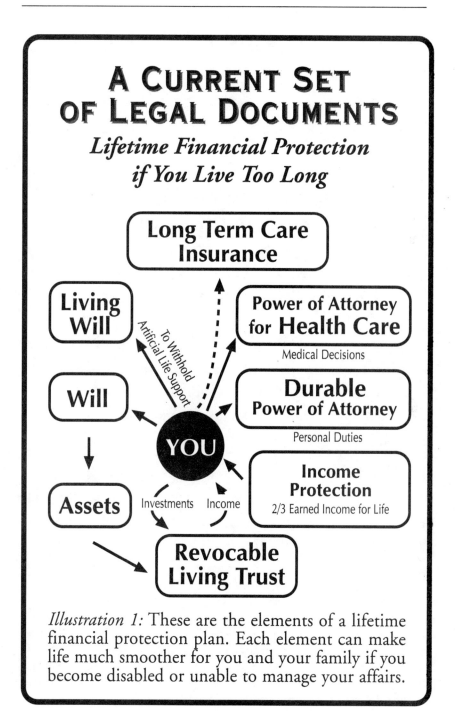

A CURRENT SET OF LEGAL DOCUMENTS

Lifetime Financial Protection if You Live Too Long

Long Term Care Insurance

Living Will

To Withhold Artificial Life Support

Power of Attorney for Health Care

Medical Decisions

Will

Durable Power of Attorney

Personal Duties

YOU

Assets

Investments   Income

Income Protection

2/3 Earned Income for Life

Revocable Living Trust

Illustration 1: These are the elements of a lifetime financial protection plan. Each element can make life much smoother for you and your family if you become disabled or unable to manage your affairs.

COMMON ERRORS TO AVOID WITH WILLS

Not everyone is careless with wills. Marilyn Monroe may have been in unbearable pain when she took an overdose of sleeping pills, but the care she took in providing for those close to her ought to serve as an inspiration for the rest of us. Monroe established a $100,000 trust to maintain the institutional care of her mentally ill mother, then left the major portion to her acting mentor, Lee Strasberg. Her psychiatrist, Marianne Kris, also inherited a share. The more than $1 million a year the estate receives in licensing fees for the use of Marilyn's image now goes to Strasberg's widow, whom he married six years after Monroe's death, and a London children's psychiatric institute, at the request of Kris.[5] You might want to keep that good will and proper planning in mind when you consider the following will-related mistakes most folks make:

ERROR # 1:

Not Having A Will. Newspapers and magazines are quick to tell us when famous people die without a will (intestate). The results are usually disastrous.[6]

---

5 Brown, *Administration of Trusts and Estates*, p. 136.

6 A dramatic instance is described by John Pletz, in "Lack of Will To Cost Inlow Estate Millions," *Indianapolis Business Journal*, July 7-13, 1997. John Inlow, age 46, died abruptly when he was struck on the head by a company helicopter. As a business lawyer for Canseco, he apparently had made millions in paper profit by exercising their stock options. Yet, he didn't have a will (or an estate tax plan, according to this article). It may cost his estate more than one-fourth of its assets. He should have known better.

Most people are aware that Howard Hughes died intestate. Lawyers (who are among his biggest heirs) fought off dozens of claims for years. Presently, more than 100 people share his estate worth about $2 billion.[7] It's just fortunate that he had enough foresight to create the Howard Hughes Medical Institute, which may have the bulk of his fortune.

Although Mr. Hughes showed us what typically happens when there is poor planning, sometimes the results aren't quite so turbulent. Consider Jerry McMorris, owner of the Colorado Rockies, whose father, Don McMorris, died in 1990 without a will.[8] When the IRS wanted to assess "extra" estate taxes of $25 million on the transfer of a family trucking business, Jerry McMorris disputed this contention. He argued his case and reportedly settled for a payment of "only" $3.8 million.[9] It's unfortunate, however, that this matter became public knowledge. The sad part is that with proper estate documents, the McMorris family might have managed this entire matter in private, without media scrutiny.

When Pablo Picasso died without a will in 1973, efforts to settle his large estate required the assistance of lawyers, appraisers, catalogers, government-appointed art experts, officials of several government ministries and the President of France. It cost his six heirs $30 million and took six years

7 Source: "The Richest People In America," *The Forbes 400.*

8 Ann Imse, "Rockies Owner Settles IRS Dispute," *Rocky Mountain News*, Jan. 31, 1996, p. 4a.

9 See Ann Imse, "Morris Pays 15% in Tax Case," *Rocky Mountain News*, February 2, 1996, p. 56a.

to reach a settlement satisfactory to all.[10]

My recommendation: Visit with a lawyer about drafting a will! Then, sign and be consistent about keeping it up-to-date.

ERROR #2:

An Out-Of-Date Will. Most wills are locked up and forgotten after they're signed. It's the rare person who can describe with much certainty what's contained in his or her will.

No one likes to discuss death and taxes, but everyone should want to protect for their heirs what took a lifetime of hard work to create. The only way this can be assured is to review matters periodically as things change during this journey we call life.

When any of the following events occur, you should review and probably change your will:

- marriage or divorce;
- birth, adoption or death of a child or grandchild;
- marriage of a child;
- death of your spouse;
- increase or decrease in net worth from a gift or inheritance;
- displeasure with the actions or lifestyle of a descendant;
- a parent or child now has special needs;
- participation in a qualified retirement plan; or

---

10 Brown, *Administration of Trusts and Estates,* p. 46.

· a move to a new state.

ERROR # 3:

Not Having A Well-Written Will. It actually may be better not to have a will at all than to have a poorly-written one. Consider the inadequacy of U.S. Supreme Court Chief Justice Warren Burger's will and the extra expense and taxes this cost his descendants.

Apparently, Mr. Burger hastily used a computer to type a one-page will (misspelling a word or two in the process.) His will didn't grant permission to sell real estate, the executors had to post an expensive bond, and there may have been improper witnessing under Virginia law. Experts aptly noted that he might have saved some $450,000 in estate and inheritance taxes if he'd just taken some more time to do it right.[11]

Warren Burger is an example of the adage, "A lawyer who represents himself has a fool for a client." Strange events occur when you "end run" the system and throw together a homemade set of estate documents.

---

11 "Ex-justice Leaves a Slapdash Will," by the Associated Press, *The Denver Post,* Nov. 1, 1995. According to lawyer Herbert Nass, both the late Jerry Garcia (Grateful Dead) and attorney William Kunstler didn't pay much attention to their wills either. Garcia's will misspelled his daughter's name; it didn't establish a $600,000 exemption trust and it named his lawyer executor. Kunstler's will didn't mention two children from a first marriage. (Unfortunately, they'll never know whether he intended to exclude them). It's apparent to Mr. Nass that wills are "the last thing on many people's minds." If so, he suggests a big party with champagne and caviar in one's final weeks as a method of beating the estate taxes. Maybe he's right. See Douglas Martin, "Some Celebrity Swan Songs Are Way Out Of Tune," *The New York Times,* May 12, 1996.

My recommendation: Read up on matters, get good legal help, and don't worry about the cost. Remember that you usually get exactly what you pay for!

ERROR # 4:

Adult Children Without Wills. I've seen some excellent estate plans pushed to the edge just because adult children didn't complete their own documents during the wealth preservation process. Consider the following circumstances:

You make significant gifts of stock in a family business to your adult son and daughter. Your son passes away without a will, and his estate is returned to you under the laws of intestacy. *The result:* Your estate tax base is increased due to this unexpected inheritance. Or, if you make gifts to children from a former marriage, some of these assets may pass to your former spouse when the child dies without a will.

My recommendation: Have another lawyer confer with children about their wills whenever you complete or update your own estate documents. Ideally, everyone should sign papers that won't return assets directly to you if your child dies first. Instead, your children might, for example, leave these assets to a trust that includes you as a beneficiary but which doesn't tax trust property as part of your estate.

ERROR # 5:

Exposing Joint Assets And Trust Property To Claims Of The Creditors. Review the clause in your will that "pays" your just debts. In your state, do these also include loans or mortgages on non-probatable joint property, or assets in trust where you are a trustee? If so, then perhaps this will should only pay down debts on assets that you own personally.

Pay attention also to the effect of language that is likely to cause insurance beneficiaries and heirs to argue over money. Let's say you owe $300,000 to Mary, a former spouse, and you've purchased a $500,000 insurance policy in an irrevocable trust (ILIT) that names your present spouse as beneficiary. This policy is collaterally assigned to cover Mary's claim, and you anticipate the trust will have a balance of $200,000 at your death. If your will pays *all* just debts, will an ILIT trustee say that personal assets must satisfy the debt to Mary? (After all, he or she wants to protect its full $500,000 for trust beneficiaries.) *The result:* If children are beneficiaries under your will; the issue is whether or not they'll owe Mary $300,000. Everything depends on how the will is written.

My recommendation: Whenever insurance benefits are assigned and payable to a personal creditor, have a lawyer determine whether the debt payment clause in your will provides that personal assets will satisfy this obligation nonetheless. If so, perhaps you should change the wording to more clearly indicate your wishes.

ERROR # 6:

Having A Poor "Tax Apportionment" Clause. A well-crafted will usually has a "catch-all" clause that leaves everything else or the "residue" to children in equal shares. This is called a residuary clause and generally, these assets pay estate taxes before final distribution of the property. This can bring about some very undesirable results.

Let's assume you have a $2 million estate consisting of a $1 million business and another $1 million in miscellaneous property. The estate taxes are $588,000, and you intend to treat your children equally. Your will leaves the business ($1 million) to your son, and the $1 million "residue" to your daughter after taxes.

Will children be treated equally? Unfortunately, no! Your daughter will receive $412,000 ($1 million less $588,000) because her one-half bears the full burden of the estate taxes.

Or, let's say you make significant taxable gifts and pay a relatively low gift tax. When these "adjusted gifts" are added to the taxable estate, there is an extra estate tax. Who pays this? It all depends on the tax apportionment clause. Consider this example:

You have a $2 million estate. Just before your death, you give $1 million to your son, and pay the gift tax of $153,000. Your will leaves remaining assets to your daughter. However, when you die, your son's gift increases the estate tax base to $2 million. (Only growth on this gift is removed from the taxable estate.) As a result, estate taxes are $435,000 ($588,000 less a gift tax of $153,000). Who pays the tax of $435,000-your son or daughter, or both? It all depends on the tax apportionment clause.

If a tax apportionment clause is ambiguous, courts will attempt to create an equitable result for the heirs. But, of course, it's better to clear this up in your will. Otherwise, you leave your children in a position to argue over money.

ERROR # 7:

No Guardian For Minor Children. When there are minor children, and both parents die, the court appoints their guardian. Unless you identify these person(s) in your wills, it may be a judge that decides who guides your children through their formative years.

My recommendation: Discuss this matter with the adults you choose to be the children's guardians. You may wish to reciprocate with close friends or relatives and agree to be guardian(s) for their children. Then create an insurance trust fund that provides for the care of your children. It's usually a good idea to provide money to permit your guardian personally to add on or build a larger home that includes their extended family.

ERROR # 8:

No Letter Of Instructions. Have you written your children a "last letter" and given them an explanation and location of your assets? This letter of instructions is not legally binding, but it clarifies matters and any further requests to be carried out. An instructive letter regarding funeral arrangements is appreciated during this difficult time. For example, you might request cremation or services in a particular church, synagogue or facility. It can even be a good idea to pay for the event while you're alive. That way, children are spared the need to second guess your wishes.[12] That doesn't

---

12 You certainly don't want anyone digging up your casket and removing it from the grave site. See Dick Cady, "Bob Irsay Rests, But Feud Over Grave Site Keeps It From Being In Peace," *The Indianapolis Star,* April 20, 1997, where Mr. Irsay's wife,

mean you can count on the living to follow through, how-ever. Charles Dickens made a point of stating in his will that he wanted a quiet, private "unostentatious" send off. He didn't want a public announcement or those attending his funeral to be dressed in mourning. All his wishes were disregarded; the funeral was a very public, showy event.[13]

ERROR # 9:

Disregarding Disclaimers. It's possible to disclaim in-herited assets and pass them to others without being taxed on the gift or bequest. Let's suppose you (the disclaimant) inherit property that you don't really need. If you accept this property and then gift it, there may be a gift tax as part of the transaction. By properly disclaiming this bequest, it passes to the next in line, and there's no transfer tax to pay.

Here are some of the requirements of a valid disclaimer under tax law:

· It must be in writing, and a representative of the es-tate must receive the notice of disclaimer within nine months of your benefactor's death (or nine months of your 21st birth-day, if later).

· You cannot accept any interest or benefit from the disclaimed property.

· Depending on your preference, a portion or all of the

Nancy, contemplates this possibility. She believes this could happen because his trustees refused to pay for the burial plot due to a feud over handling of her husband's assets. This appears to be just another case about money. Is it really the "root of all evil?"

13 Brown, *Administration of Trusts and Estates,* p. 100.

bequest can be disclaimed.

· You cannot designate who receives this property. The disclaimed assets under the will pass as if a disclaimant predeceased the deceased.

Obviously, the "rub" with disclaimers is that your disclaimant has no control over who receives the property. *My recommendation:* If you believe your children might disclaim a bequest, ask them who should inherit it instead. An alternative possibility is a trust for your grandchild. By discussing this now, your family works together and everyone knows what to expect.

ERROR # 10:

Leaving Assets To "Issue" And Disinheriting An Adopted Heir. When you leave property to "issue," you create a legal group of heirs that in most states includes only natural born descendants. This may cause an unfortunate situation.

For instance, let's say you leave a residuary estate to "issue, per stirpes," meaning that the natural born children of a deceased child takes their share. There are two children, and one of them predeceases you, leaving an adopted son. *The result:* Your child's adopted child is excluded from an inheritance.[14]

---

14 Elvis Presley's will contained a testamentary trust directing the trustee to pay for support and maintenance of his daughter, Lisa Marie Presley and "any other lawful issue I might have." Deborah Delaine Presley filed a petition alleging that she was the illegitimate daughter of Elvis Presley and therefore, deserving of a share of the estate. The court, however, determined that the question of paternity was beyond the scope of its proceeding. Brown, *Administration of Estates*, p. 9.

My recommendation: If you intend to treat adopted and natural born descendants alike, ask a lawyer to be sure they aren't inadvertently disinherited.

ERROR # 11:

Not Having Enough Of The Right Witnesses. Since most states require three persons to witness the signing of a will, it's best to routinely have three, rather than two, people sign as witnesses whenever you make changes to your will. These should be people you know and not merely employees in a lawyer's office. If any of your witnesses ever has to testify that you possessed sound mind and memory to make a will, it's best for them to have been acquainted with you personally.[15]

It's also best not to select a witness who will inherit under the will. It's likely that a witness—inheritor cannot testify regarding your competence, the validity of a signature, or even the soundness of the will itself.

ERROR # 12:

Setting Your Estate Up For A Will Contest. It seems that disgruntled family members are more likely than ever these days to contest a will. Consider these grounds for over-turning a will:

A.   You were not of sound mind or memory (not knowing the extent of your holdings and the objects of your

---

15 When George Washington prepared his will in his own handwriting, no witnesses were necessary because a handwritten testament without them was considered binding, back in the 1790s in the first President's home state. Brown, *Administration of Estates*, p 113.

bounty).

B.   Someone has attempted to unduly influence you to make a will, or there is a mistake in the will.[16]

C.   You didn't follow the formalities the law required for making a will (witnesses, signatures, declarations, style, etc., as required by your state).

There are several circumstances that actually seem to encourage others to argue that a will should be overturned. Let's say you disinherit a child (or even a spouse[17]) or leave more to one than another, or you favor a second spouse or lover over children from a first marriage (or even if you favor the children).[18] You may even expect trouble if most of the

---

16 When artist Georgia O'Keefe died at age 98, leaving an estate worth over $70 million, excluded family members contested her will. They argued that Jaun Hamilton, a male assistant more than 50 years younger than O'Keefe, unduly influenced her. O'Keefe had given Hamilton power of attorney eight years before she died. She originally left him her ranch and 21 paintings, then in a second codicil, more than 70 percent of her estate. Hamilton eventually agreed to a settlement with O'Keefe's sister and niece. It was never known whether his influence on the artist was a natural expression of affection on her part, or deliberate manipulation on his. Brown, *Administration of Estates*, p. 294.

17 Jack Kent Cooke, deceased former owner of the Washington Redskins wrote his wife, Marlene, out of his will 13 weeks before he died in April of 1997. His estate claims this should hold-up because Marlene violated a pre-nuptial agreement requiring her to live with Cooke as his wife. As you would expect, she now alleges that he coerced her signature and that entitles her under Virginia law to receive one-third of his $500 million to $825 million estate. See Justin Blum, "Lawyers Seek to Question Marlene Cooke About Male Friends," *Washington Post*, Dec. 9, 1997, p. B04. In the meantime, Cooke's estate wants Marlene to return 400 heirlooms and other items it believes she wrongfully removed from their family home. Justin Blum, "Marlene Cooke Sued Over Heirlooms," *Washington Post*, Dec. 13, 1997, p. B04. The beat goes on!

18 Bob Magness left his second wife, Sharon, specific bequests of at least $35 million, *The Last Will And Testament Of Bob Magness*. But she wants more of his $1

estate is left to charity.[19] The following ideas minimize the chances of a will contest:

·   Have three individuals that you know personally witness your will, and do not include them as beneficiaries.

·   If you are philanthropic, create a charitable trust(s) while you're alive, and make it an operating entity. Having established this clear philanthropic intention, then have your will leave a charitable bequest to this trust(s).

·   If you favor one heir over another, include an explanation in your will.[20] Better yet: Treat all heirs fairly and equally under the will. Then, to do something special for one of them, make a gift or establish a special trust arrangement for him or her while you're alive.

·   Consider a clause in your will or trust that removes a

billion estate, and she is suing in probate court to get it. See John Accola, "$50 Million Is Not Enough For Wife," *Rocky Mountain News,* July 18, 1997, p. 1B. Seward Johnson left most of his fortune to Basia, his third wife. In one of the most bitter will contests ever, six children from two previous marriages challenged his bequests. This case was filled with scandal, adultery, drugs and murder plots. Sometimes money brings out the worst in people. See David Margolick, *Undue Influence* (Morrow & Company, Inc., 1993).

19 Eleanor Ritchey, heiress of the Quaker State Refining Corporation, willed $4.5 million to her 150 dogs in 1968. Family members contested the will, and the escrow increased to $14 million in the meantime. Ultimately, the family received $2 million; the 73 dogs who were still alive received $123,287.69 each for food, grooming and housing ($9 million in total) and the $3 million remaining was spent on legal fees. Brown, *Administration of Estates,* p. 132.

20 Explanations can't always prevent feuds, but they are worth the effort. When Henry Ford II created his will, he was so intent of keeping the peace in his family that he left a videotape to be shown after his death. In it, he explained to his third wife, and his three children from his first marriage why he distributed his $325 million estate as he did. Even that, however, wasn't enough to prevent a feud between his wife and the children, who had earlier demonstrated their animosity by boycotting the couple's wedding. Brown, *Administration of Estates,* p. 4.

contesting beneficiary from inheriting under the document.[21] Although not valid in all states, this language increases the stakes when someone is considering a will contest.

·   Take the preparation and execution of your will seriously. It's a valuable privilege under the law. Be as clear and specific as possible regarding bequests of property.

·   Select a personal representative carefully. Sometimes heirs aren't pleased with persons named to administer an estate. Consequently, they begin a lawsuit or a will contest to seek the removal of this individual.[22]

·   Use a revocable trust as a will substitute. A proposed executor or personal representative must be approved by the heirs, but the trustee of a revocable living trust simply continues in that capacity with no consent is required.

REVOCABLE LIVING TRUSTS

It has been said that trusts are the most important gifts bestowed by the English legal system on modern America. I

---

21 In Bob Irsay's will, there is a stipulation that beneficiaries who challenge it will not inherit from the estate, according to Welton W. Harris II, in "Lawyer Says Nancy Irsay's Inheritance In Jeopardy," *The Indianapolis Star*, Jan., 25, 1997. At least Chicago attorney Daniel W. Luther apparently took this position after Mrs. Irsay attempted to remove five persons named by her husband as executors.

22 When Doris Duke, the tobacco heiress died in 1993, her will made the butler, Bernard Lafferty, her unlikely executor of the estate (and gave him a key role, as well, in the charitable foundation formed to manage most of her assets). After huge legal fees and a flurry of charges and counter-charges, Mr. Lafferty died in November of 1996, and most of the complications ended. Unfortunately, much of this dispute was probably avoidable if Mrs. Duke had only selected a professional independent representative (or trustee) for her estate. See Matthew Purdy, "Attorneys cash in on complexities of billionaire's will-Estate designated for charity; legal fees at $10 million," *The New York Times*, Feb. 2, 1997.

agree. Today, it's common for lawyers and financial advisors to routinely suggest trusts as part of an estate plan. In some parts of the country, salespersons actually "market" these arrangements for the protection of assets for future generations.[23]

A trust is merely an arrangement where someone (a trust creator) transfers assets to an intermediary (a trustee) who manages this property for others (a beneficiary). U.S. law holds these arrangements in such high regard that trust documents can even shelter property for a spendthrift beneficiary and from the unfortunate circumstances of a lawsuit. *The result:* Trusts protect assets more than any other form of property ownership.

For our purposes, I'll define an RLT as a trust established by a creator during his or her lifetime. The creator is trustee and beneficiary.[24] It can be canceled, modified or amended, and it typically ends at the creator's death when trust assets are included in the deceased's estate tax base.

23 Be aware, however, of the so-called "cure-all" equity trust that is carefully packaged and marketed to unsuspecting purchasers. See James Ingraham, Esq., "The Pure Equity Trust: A Tax Time Bomb for the Unwary," *The Colorado Lawyer*, April, 1997, Vol. 26, No. 4, p. 47; and Jan M. Rosen, "A Trust Or A Trap? The IRS Wants To Know," *The New York Times*, May 25, 1997 where the author explains that the IRS may seek criminal charges against participants and promoters of trusts that promise too much in the way of income and estate tax savings. Also, in IRS Notice 97-24, there are five examples of "abusive" trusts, namely, the Business Trust, the Equipment or Service Trust, the Family Residence Trust, the Charitable Trust and the Final Trust. Each arrangement promises unusual benefits not common to legitimate trusts sometimes bearing these names.

24 Know that as a general rule, it is not possible to gain creditor and lawsuit protection for a creator if he or she is beneficiary of the trust. This benefit is only available for other recipients.

Don't get me wrong; RLTs aren't a cure-all for a weak estate strategy.[25] Like all planning, it's necessary to pay close attention to the rules when you create a trust. Because so much is at stake, a perfectly innocent arrangement can still be a breeding ground for lawsuits that pit trustee against beneficiary, or even beneficiary against beneficiary if one believes the other has received the better arrangement.

Here are some traps you'll want to avoid:

TRAP # 1:

Not Having A Living Trust. Trusts can be complicated. If you have a low tolerance for planning, you may believe the answer is a "simple will" that leaves everything directly to your spouse or heirs. This brief document basically avoids "legalese," and it may seem preferable to a more comprehensive set of legal papers. But, I tend to disagree.

It's true that trusts are more expensive and complex than simple wills which transfer property outright. However, when a creative attorney prepares an RLT, it will win every time over a simple will. Here's how:

· An RLT that holds assets won't come under public scrutiny. In most states, it mostly maintains privacy and even secrecy for the family[26] by sidestepping the probate process.

---

25 RLTs aren't even a complete substitute for a will that should be signed in all instances. See Thomas L. Stover, "Ten Good Reasons *Not* To Avoid Colorado Probate," *The Colorado Lawyer*, Sept., 1996, Vol. 25, No. 9, p. 69.

26 When TCI Chairman, Bob Magness died in 1996 (apparently *without a funded RLT*), Colorado probate lawyer William Huff moved quickly to seal the $1 billion estate from public scrutiny. He said that to explain why would "let the cat out of the bag." The judge agreed but said this matter would be revisited in three months. See

- Because of better settled law, RLTs are superior to limited durable powers of attorney when it comes to managing the property of a disabled person.[27] Securities firms and others are usually more friendly when asked to deal with a trustee.

- An RLT may better withstand a challenge to its validity than a will.

- RLTs give you an opportunity to get acquainted with the plan you are making for family. You can even be trustee personally and call a living trust a "trial run," if you prefer.

- To some extent, RLTs save and shorten the probate process (which essentially is a lawsuit you file against yourself, and you lose). This is sometimes only a minor advantage, however, since most states have now streamlined and reduced the cost of this matter. If you have real property in several states, an RLT will probably save considerably on probate costs. If a trust owns this property, there's no reason to have a proceeding in each location just to change title.[28]

Stephen Keating, "No Public Scrutiny for Magness Estate," *Denver Post*, Dec. 21, 1996. Three months later, the whole matter was debated again. The estate's lawyers requested another six months of privacy; media attorneys for two major newspapers, however, argued that the records should be unsealed immediately. See John Accola, "Attorneys Try to Keep Magness Will Secret," *Rocky Mountain News*, March 21, 1997, p. 10.

27 Consider the unfortunate Groucho Marx story as explained by Robert A. Esperti and Renno L. Peterson, in *Loving Trust*, (Viking, 1988, p. 88.) In his declining years, Groucho was declared mentally incompetent. He and his personal affairs were paraded before the public and courts. This man and his family endured more abuse than you can possibly imagine. It was avoidable if only he had had a living trust.

28 Keep in mind, that although a funded RLT probably escapes all probate, the trusts will not avoid inheritance taxes if the state of location still levies this type of tax.

My recommendation: Spend the time and money necessary to craft a revocable living trust. I especially recommend if you're older or have assets in two or more states.[29]

Here are other errors to avoid:

TRAP # 2:

Confusing A Living Trust With Estate Tax Savings.
People who have created RLTs commonly believe they have reduced estate taxes or have even avoided the tax system altogether. An RLT is a good start to an overall wealth preservation program, but don't equate its probate protection with tax savings. Although RLTs can save taxes by sheltering $600,000 in a "bypass family trust" at death, this is also possible with a testamentary trust (a trust that isn't created until a will becomes effective). An RLT doesn't save taxes; it just creates a tax-friendly structure. In other words, trusts avoid probate, but tax planning is still necessary.

TRAP # 3:

Failure To Fund A Living Trust. RLTs can involve expensive legal and financial fees. All too often, however, these documents are signed without funding the trust. Many people believe they will get around to this someday, but someday turns out to be too late!

My recommendation: An RLT is a protective wealth preservation device, and once signed you should transfer per-

---

29 For an excellent book on living trusts, read Robert A. Esperti and Renno L. Petersen, *The Living Trust Revolution,* (Viking, 1992.) This interesting work explains in lay person terms how living trusts can help (or possibly hinder) your wealth preservation plan.

sonal assets to it immediately. Since a good trust lawyer will give full instructions, there's no excuse for not following them.

TRAP # 4:

Confusing An "Equity" Trust With A Revocable Living Trust. For years, a brand of living trust has been marketed under the name "Constitutional Trust," Sovereign Trust," "Unincorporated Business Organization" ("UBO") and others, including a recent version referred to as an "Equity Trust."[30] In general, this trust establishes "units of beneficial interest" which purport to make certain trust benefits available to its creator.

In a nutshell, equity trusts are sold door-to-door and promote the transfer of assets to a trust before death to avoid probate, lawyer's fees, executor's fees and more. Here's where they really get interesting: These structures promise that you can use and control trust property without paying income or transfer taxes; even creditor-proofing is offered as an extra benefit.

CAUTION: The IRS has indicated that equity trusts should be avoided. Numerous rulings contradict the benefits promised. Indeed, the government views these arrangements as fraudulent schemes to evade taxes. There are substantial penalties - even criminal sanctions - risked by trust promoters and participants.

My recommendation: It's possible that mass-marketed trusts are shams and tax abusive arrangements. If you hear about "living trusts" that seem too good to be true, they probably

30 See note 23 *supra.*

are. Take the promotional information to a trusted advisor for scrutiny.

TRAP # 5:

Living Trusts That Terminate At The Creator's Death. For some reason, many living trusts end at the creator's death. How unfortunate! When a trust terminates at the creator's death, it's apparent that the trust document was prepared for only three reasons - to save probate costs, maintain privacy, and to manage assets if there's a disability. While these are noble motives, your family is shortchanged unless the RLT is extended to benefit at least your spouse and children during their lifetimes. Remember that it's always easier to terminate a trust that isn't working than it is to begin a new estate plan.

Our legal system blesses trust arrangements that are arranged for other people. When a trust terminates, the planning must begin anew, and that's not always easy to accomplish. When the period is extended, a carefully crafted trust manages assets and shelters them from lawsuits, failed marriages and family conflict for the duration. That's something you can't really do when you receive assets outright.

My recommendation: Once you go to the expense, time and effort to create an RLT, specify that it continues for your family.

TRAP # 6:

Not Extending This Trust If There Is Danger. So, you still wish that trust assets could belong to your children outright. It's one thing to terminate an RLT and turn over the assets to children directly; it's a travesty to do this if these assets are immediately gobbled up by a creditor, predator, a lawsuit, or a spouse in an unfriendly divorce. It may be possible to extend a terminating RLT if these dangers are threatened or pending. *My recommendation:* If you don't want to extend an RLT, at least give the trustee power to continue it until all seas are calm.

GOING OUT IN STYLE

When financier J.P. Morgan died in 1913, his will provided one year's salary to each employee of J.P. Morgan and Company. Joseph Pulitzer also left most of his fortune to his employees. His faithful valet received the equivalent of $325,000 in current dollars; his chief secretary over $260,000 and his "oldest and most faithful employees at the two newspapers he owned, got to divide $40,000 among them.

Katherine Saunders, a Norwood, Massachusetts poet, left this poem when she died in 1992, at the age of 86:[31]

Spare Parts

They're waiting around for my kidneys;
They're eager to get at my eyes
They covet my liver and look on the giver
as taking her time when she dies

They grin in anticipation
Do you s'pose her kidneys will "take"?
Her arm or her heart or some other part
What lovely skin grafts she'll make.

---

31 Brown, *Administration of Trusts and Estates,* p.366.

CHAPTER 9

IRREVOCABLE
LIFE INSURANCE TRUSTS
(ILITs):

TRUSTS THAT OWN
TAX-FREE LIFE INSURANCE

I In Chapter 7, you learned how to design a life insurance portfolio to your advantage. In most cases, it's best to make an Irrevocable Life Insurance Trust (ILIT) owner-beneficiary of all policies. Used correctly, an ILIT can be a key element in a wealth preservation plan. But you have to know how to manage it properly; otherwise you'll undo all the good you've set out to accomplish. We'll look at how to keep them problem-free in this chapter.

For our purposes, let's define the ILIT as a trust created by an insured (who cannot cancel it or modify its terms). While the creator is alive, the beneficiaries are spouse and family. The primary purpose of an ILIT is to eliminate insurance proceeds from the insured's estate tax base. At death, the trustee loans cash to (or uses it to acquire assets from) an estate's personal representative. (See Illustration #1.) Then the trust ends, and assets are distributed to adult children. If a share belongs to a minor, it is held until the beneficiary reaches age 21.

I find it unfortunate that more successful people haven't taken such steps to guarantee liquidity for their heirs or charity. There are really only two planning possibilities – provide protective liquidity for the estate or sell its valuable assets to pay the tax.

Life insurance provides the "glue" that can keep an estate together (or replace assets given to those less fortunate). Just as obtaining a key person policy is one cost of doing business[1], so is obtaining an individual policy the price of preserving family wealth. It makes sense, therefore, to gift insurance contracts to an ILIT[2], which will shelter them from transfer taxes, and debts of the estate. Unfortunately, it takes a certain amount of care to keep these wonderful structures from totally falling apart. Let's look more closely at what this entails. Here are common mistakes you'll want to avoid.

MISTAKES TO AVOID

MISTAKE # 1:

Not having an ILIT. Back in Chapter 7, I told you it's

---

1 See Chapter 3, "Family Business Planning."

2 The gift tax cost of premiums is relatively low in comparison to the estate tax cost on death proceeds. Also, gifts of other assets may cause a loss in basis step-up at death. With income tax-free insurance, the loss of basis step-up is of no concern. Finally, life insurance is an easy gift, psychologically, since it is generally considered post-death security for others.

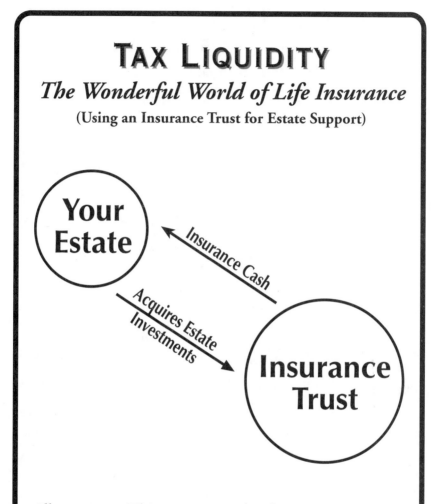

TAX LIQUIDITY
The Wonderful World of Life Insurance
(Using an Insurance Trust for Estate Support)

Illustration 1: This is an example of an Insurance Trust consisting of *cash* proceeds (no estate or income taxes) which purchase *assets* from your *estate*.

The insurance cash pays estate taxes or fulfills a bequest to charity. If the *trust* continues for generations to come, its assets are never estate taxed again. Trust property is protected from the creditors and failed marriages of your beneficiaries, according to the terms of the document.

usually best to place a life insurance policy in a trust when the coverage is meant to benefit family. This protects the contract when an insured is alive, and rescues insurance money otherwise subject to estate tax at death. Let's look at this in some detail.

The tax law includes *proceeds* of insurance—and not the cash value—in an owner-insured's estate tax base. Therefore, if one goal is transfer tax savings, always designate an appropriate "other" to own your insurance policies.[3]

Let's say you gift a policy to a son, Marty, who makes it payable to "your estate." The estate representative has money for taxes and costs, but this doesn't save the estate tax. Tax law traps the proceeds as if you owned the contract personally. This is because the beneficiary is your estate.

Does it help if you make Marty the beneficiary, with a legal understanding that he is fully obligated to pay your death taxes? Not if you want to avoid estate taxes. This still traps proceeds in the estate tax base. But that's not the only problem. Marty may not want to remit the taxes he was "obligated" to pay. The result: The estate sells its assets at an auction.[4]

To resolve this, create an ILIT and provide a clause that a

---

3 It's not enough to give away the face amount and keep merely the cash values, and as I'll explain, your 51 percent "controlled" corporation can't own these cash values either. It's not even sufficient to gift the contract and keep a right to borrow against the policy or assign it for a loan. (Although apparently merely keeping rights to policy dividends does not confer an ownership right, I don't recommend this strategy. The conservative approach is to give up all control over the policy.)

4 For example, see Chapter 1 "Apathy, Torpor and Procrastination," Note 21 that describes the Sammy Davis Jr. auction for the sale of family heirlooms.

trustee may merely (1) loan insurance proceeds to your estate, or (2) use this money to acquire property from the personal representative. Then the cash is available for taxes, but it doesn't artificially increase the estate tax base.

MISTAKE # 2:

Waiting too long to create an ILIT. People who acquire life insurance in their 20s or 30s, don't tend to have large holdings in non-insurance property. They'll probably prefer to own the cash values in insurance policies— especially for emergencies, educational costs, and even for retirement later in life. But there is a better way. Create an ILIT that potentially provides insureds and beneficiaries indirect access to these funds, while the creator is alive. Here's how:

To gain an estate tax advantage, the insured must *irrevocably* gift all policy ownership rights. This means you must part with the authority to amend, modify, or alter the ILIT. You can't even be trustee or a beneficiary in case of an emergency. But this doesn't have to stop you from keeping a modest "string" on trust assets. Here's how a creative lawyer might write the trust document to give some indirect control:

   ·   "The trustee has authority to make distributions to your spouse, children and grandchildren." The trustee may also loan money to anyone *including you.* (During your lifetime, the trustee borrows cash values and pays or loans them as indicated.)

   ·   "A beneficiary or a beneficiary-trustee has authority to take distributions for himself, (or herself) for expenses related to their health, education, maintenance and support— so-called `HEMS' power." Be aware, however, that the trust must also bar payments that fulfill a duty of support on the part of the insured or a spouse. (During your lifetime, a beneficiary obtains cash values or distributes them to family for HEMS –they voluntarily join with you to enjoy these funds.)

·   "A spouse is defined as a wife (or husband) to whom a beneficiary (or insured) is married at any time during continuance of this trust." (If you divorce and remarry, a new spouse steps into this definition in the trust document, and may become a beneficiary of trust funds.)

The problem: Once you create an ILIT, there can be no guarantee that you'll be able to use the trust's cash values.

My recommendation: Remedy this is with a well-crafted agreement (and a little imagination), that allows you to indirectly enjoy every last dollar in the trust—and then some.

MISTAKE # 3:

No "trap doors" to change or cancel the trust. Obviously, an ILIT can make payments to a "spouse" and family for most any reason. However, there is still a possibility that the trust won't work for you. Perhaps there has been a breakup in the family, or some other change that makes the beneficiary setup less than ideal. To solve these problems, an ILIT should have "trap doors"[5] that permit you to start over. Here

---

5 "ILIT trap doors" are terms I'll attribute to Rich Elrod, a marvelous estate planning lawyer in Denver, Colorado. He frequently mentioned this possibility in his estate planning meetings. In April, 1997, Rich died unexpectedly at age 47; his many, many clients and friends miss him greatly.

is some trust language that can accomplish this:

· "An independent trustee (perhaps a friend) can sell a policy to anyone, including the trust-creator." Just be sure you don't have the legal right to buy the policies insuring your life. (The trustee sells the policies to you for cash then terminates the trust and distributes money to the beneficiary.)

· "An independent trustee can distribute a policy to a spouse or another beneficiary for any reason." (The trustee turns over a policy, and the trust is terminated.)

· "A beneficiary or a beneficiary-trustee can withdraw a policy for his or her health, education, maintenance or support —HEMS." (The trustee turns over a policy and notes the reason.)

· "An independent trustee, or a trust protector —perhaps a friend— can amend, reform or terminate the trust, or transfer assets to a new trust created by the insured." (The trustee turns over the policy and the trust is terminated.)

Finally, if all beneficiaries agree, a trustee can usually terminate the trust unless this defeats the creator's original reason for establishing it. (The trustee should always ask for a family settlement agreement that protects everyone when the trust no longer exists.)

As you can see, there are strategies to indirectly access assets in an ILIT. You just have to use creative thinking and work within the law. Even if the trap doors fail, you can always stop making premium-gifts. The trustee will make an adjustment in the policy and it will eventually be canceled due to lack of funds.

MISTAKE # 4:

Originating the insurance policy incorrectly. As with any complex strategy, it is possible to make a mistake, especially at the beginning when the insurance is acquired. Even timing can be critical. Here's why:

For years, the IRS has been concerned with its loss of tax revenue that occurs when someone in poor health acquires an insurance policy and transfers it to another person (or trust). If that individual dies shortly afterwards, the proceeds escape estate taxes. To avoid this lost revenue, the law gives an estate tax break only if an insured lives three years after the transfer of a policy.

Of course, with the gift of an old policy, the three-year period probably begins when a transfer of ownership form is signed and mailed to the insurance company. That raises the following question: "How do you acquire a new ILIT policy without falling into the three year transfer trap?" Here are the possibilities:

· You apply for a policy and bind it with a premium. The trust is signed. Then the ILIT is established. Once a policy is approved it is transferred to the trust. Unfortunately, this transfer begins the three-year period.

· The trust isn't signed, but you and the trustee have a verbal understanding of the arrangement. Your "trustee-owner" signs the application and you bind it with a premium. When the policy is approved, the trust is signed (and dated back to when the application was taken). Some planners believe a transfer problem is avoided when there is this clear verbal understanding that a trust is created and it applies for insurance. Others disagree. They say that a trust can't be that specific unless it is written. Personally, I don't recommend relying on an oral trust approach.

·   The trust isn't signed, and you apply for a policy (for underwriting purposes only). No binder is taken. When the trust is signed later, a trustee writes a new application. A premium is paid when the policy is approved. The IRS has ruled that there is no transfer problem when you follow this procedure.

·   The trust is signed, and it applies for your policy. A binder is taken. Courts have ruled that there is no transfer using this approach.

My recommendation: Have a trust prepared before an application is taken. Then sign the paperwork and bind the policy. If the trust must be delayed, however, apply for a policy personally and bind it. Then transfer it to the trust later, and just accept the fact that you've got a three-year wait before you can be assured of a tax break. If you are concerned about estate taxes, purchase additional term life insurance for three years. (Some insurers provide this coverage automatically for last survivor policies owned by an ILIT.)

MISTAKE # 5:

Selecting a trust document "off the shelf." Fight the tendency to sign a "boilerplate" irrevocable trust document, in haste. If the ILIT can't be tailored to your special circumstances, for some reason or another, communicate your intentions clearly to counsel. Here are some special trust provisions that aren't always included in boilerplate paperwork. They take extra effort, but can be very helpful:

· Include the "trap doors" referred to in this chapter.

· Give beneficiaries rights to withdraw contributions from all sources. (This makes it possible for grandparents and other relatives to also make transfers that qualify as $10,000 annual gifts.)

· Outline a written procedure for guardians to withdraw gifts intended for minor beneficiaries.

· Don't require that a trustee acquire the life insurance. This discourages an IRS argument that the ILIT is merely an "agent" of the creator. For instance, a trustee is authorized (but not directed) to acquire life insurance and pay premiums. (Also, don't refer to the ILIT as an "insurance trust." It's better to simply call it a "family trust" instead.)

· "Fail-safe" this trust if for some reason its assets are still included in your estate tax base. This is accomplished by qualifying trust property for the marital deduction in that circumstance. If there is no surviving spouse, the trust simply obligates its beneficiaries to pay their share of the estate tax.

I feel strongly that an "off the shelf" document just isn't acceptable. Remember, the purpose of an ILIT is to protect life insurance benefits from estate taxes and the possibility of litigation. Since the ILIT is irrevocable, the creator cannot change it. That's why it's so important to take the extra time (and possibly the expense) to make sure the trust has all necessary provisions to suit your circumstances. Let me suggest that you also consider including language in the trust that permits a disinterested trustee or other person to amend the trust from time to time. This can add flexibility in the event circumstances change.

MISTAKE # 6:

Omitting specific insurance language within the trust.
To protect the trustee, give an ILIT some specific language relating to life insurance. Otherwise, a fiduciary can easily be liable for doing acts not authorized by the agreement. Here are some examples of how a trust document properly gives trustees special authority over insurance decisions:

· The trust can purchase single and survivorship policies of any product design including term, whole life, universal life, variable life, variable universal life (or a mixture thereof);

· A 1035 (tax-free) insurance exchange is permitted;

· There is a right to borrow or withdraw policy values;

· The trustee can surrender policies, or modify or amend face values, premium schedules or other benefits;

· There can be split-dollar arrangements—trust and trust-trust and individuals—and trust and other entities; and

· If a policy becomes a Modified Endowment Contract (MEC), the trustee is specifically relieved of liability for borrowing or withdrawing policy values that are taxable.

The problem: Most ILITs aren't creatively worded in a way that's especially oriented to life insurance strategies. *My recommendation:* Ask the insurance company to review your ILIT document, and carefully suggest insurance language that provides flexibility and protects a trustee from legal difficulties.

MISTAKE # 7:

Avoiding gift tax rules of the "game"– the Crummey rules. Your first goal is to establish an ILIT that owns life insurance that isn't subject to estate tax at death. This is a good use of tax leverage, where say a $1 million trust policy can be compared to assets worth at least $2 million in an estate (assuming a 50 percent transfer tax bracket). The next goal, typically, is to make premium-transfers without paying gift taxes, either. Keep in mind that the IRS doesn't like this any more than it believes life insurance should always be estate or income tax-free at death. Consequently, there are some special traps when your plan includes $10,000 gifts to irrevocable trusts. Here's why:

The original goal is to protect transfers up to $10,000 ($20,000 with a spouse) from gift tax, and to do this for each premium-gift made to the trust. This task is difficult because only gifts *to* someone can qualify as a tax-free. Gifts made to a trust are *for* someone, and the law taxes all gifts that can't be used presently. This is where Crummey gifts (not to be confused with transfers that just plain aren't any good) come into play.

In 1968, a taxpayer named Crummey won a case with the IRS which involved the establishment of an irrevocable trust for children. His trust gifts were tax-free because the beneficiaries (or their guardians) had 13 days each year to withdraw these payments to the trust. Since this case, tax planners refer to most ILITs as Crummey trusts when beneficiaries are given this limited withdrawal privilege. Without it, all gifts to trusts would be taxable (with no gift tax up to $600,000—and gift tax thereafter).

Crummey ILITs have become a mainstay in most wealth preservation plans. If the rules aren't followed carefully, however, premium-gifts aren't tax-free. To provide some idea of how much red tape is involved, here are the rules to follow that should clearly shelter $10,000 transfers from a gift tax payment:

- Give each beneficiary a copy of the trust;
- Have the trust state clearly how the trustee will give beneficiaries notice that they can make withdrawals—then give actual notice of a withdrawal right to the beneficiary (or a parent or guardian of a minor);[6]
- Give each beneficiary a reasonable time to withdraw (say 30 days from notice);
- Make contributions to the trust before December 1st;
- Know that the IRS doesn't approve of giving with-

---

6 The consequences of not notifying ILIT beneficiaries of withdrawal rights can cost some real tax money. EZ Notice in New York City and On Trak Administration Services Co., Inc. in Scottsdale, Arizona, are organizations that handle all of the administrative aspects of Crummey notices. If you'd like their phone number, call me at 303-756-3599.

drawal privileges to remote beneficiaries (such as distant relatives) who may not receive anything else from the trust. Although courts tend to disagree with the IRS on this issue, it's still better to provide some additional trust benefits for each beneficiary who can withdraw the premium-gifts;

   ·   In early policy years, there may be inadequate cash values to satisfy withdrawal rights permitted in the trust. Therefore, permit a beneficiary a share of the policy instead of the cash gift itself. Better yet: Ask the insurance company for a letter that they will give 30-day refunds as long as timely premiums are paid—then give notices to beneficiaries at least 30 days before premiums are actually remitted;

   ·   Document all withdrawal notices. Send them by certified mail with a return receipt requested. Or ask that beneficiaries return notices indicating a decision whether or not to withdraw; and

   ·   Don't threaten punishment to a beneficiary, who actually withdraws the cash. Just have the trust prohibit this person from participating in future withdrawals. Better yet: Let him or her continue participating. Perhaps they really needed the money that one time!

These are some key aspects of Crummey withdrawal trusts. If the rules aren't followed, anticipate that IRS will make all gifts taxable. Be aware, also, that there are always other issues when you do comprehensive Crummey ILIT planning. *My recommendation:* Select your legal and insurance advisors carefully, and interview them about how they organize a Crummey trust. It is a big mistake to treat this aspect of

ILIT planning carelessly. What's at risk is your tax-free gift, at the very least!

MISTAKE # 8:

A beneficiary contributes to an ILIT. Situations in which a beneficiary makes gifts or contributions to an irrevocable trust can create traps for the unwary. Here's why:

Let's say, for instance, you establish an ILIT that owns insurance on a spouse. As a beneficiary, too, you anticipate trust distributions eventually. Or, your spouse creates an ILIT that names you beneficiary, and both of you are insured under its second-to-die policy. Let's suppose that in each situation, you make premium-gifts to the trustee.

The problem: Technically, you've made transfers to a trust and kept a "retained life estate." As a result, the trust assets are included in your estate tax base and are taxable by law. *My recommendation:* If you are a beneficiary of an ILIT, do not make contributions to it.

MISTAKE # 9:

Foregoing a "non-Crummey" trust. I just told you why it's smart to pay close attention to the Crummey gift tax rules. But realize that the standard advice, to avoid paying tax on premium-gifts, isn't always appropriate. Sometimes it's best to make taxable gifts anyway. Here's an excellent planning idea. You'll probably laugh at the name, however. It's called an "intentionally defective trust."

Let's say you and spouse want to make $10,000 gifts directly to children and grandchildren. You take delight in sharing with them and frankly, you'd like to watch them spend (or save) the cash. However, perhaps you don't want to make Crummey trust gifts and risk their withdrawing this money.

In these situations, consider gifting your $600,000 life-time "exemptions" to the ILIT. There is no gift tax to pay and you avoid all (notice and withdrawal) complications of the Crummey rules. In addition, there is potentially a unique advantage when a trust funded with income producing property is made "intentionally defective."

Example: Let's suppose a $1.2 million gift in trust earns taxable income of $100,000 annually. Normally, the trust pays income taxes of about $40,000, and the $60,000 remaining is available for insurance premiums. However, if the ILIT is made "defective"[7] under tax law, the creator must pay all income taxes for the trust and this improves its cash flow from $60,000 to $100,000. What's more: The creator's tax payment of $40,000 isn't treated as a taxable transfer under the law in effect in 1997.

My recommendation: To simplify matters, consider making "taxable" gifts to an "intentionally defective" ILIT. Death benefits are still estate and income tax leveraged; without the complications associated with Crummey gifts. You'll pay income taxes for the trust, and under the law it appears that this is not a taxable gift to anyone. Finally, if you "need" the

---

7 A trust is "defective" if, for instance, (a) a trustee can pay life insurance premiums without any restrictions or (b) the creator can reacquire trust assets by substituting other property of equivalent value.

gifts someday, be sure a lawyer provides the indirect control or trap doors I mentioned earlier.

MISTAKE # 10:

Poor communication between trustee and beneficiaries. In chapter 7, I told you about a case in which trust beneficiaries filed a lawsuit, prompted by the fact that the insured died shortly after creating an insurance trust. At issue was whether a $50,000 premium acquired "enough" insurance.

Good communication at the outset could have prevented this. With ILITs, lawsuits are usually avoidable if the trustee uses common sense, communicates well with beneficiaries, and maintains good records. If you are this fiduciary, here are seven tips that can prevent that date in court:

1.   Ask drafting counsel for a summary that outlines key features of the ILIT agreement. Also request a letter of instructions regarding Crummey withdrawal procedures.

2.   Ask an independent party to perform an initial and occasional review of insurance policies held in the trust.

3.   Ask the insurance agent for "in-force" ledgers of all policies, annually, and compare the results to those projected initially.

4.   Keep all records pertaining to Crummey withdrawal notices.

5.   Notify beneficiaries and insured if an insurer is issued a lower financial rating.

6.   Avoid transactions which involve an apparent con-

flict of interest.

7.   Keep all insurance illustrations and notes about decisions pertaining to insurance face amounts, policy options and the intention to make premium-gifts.

MISTAKE # 11:

A creator has too much power to change trustees. If an insured-grantor of an ILIT is also trustee, insurance proceeds are included in his or her estate tax base. For this reason, the creator typically names another party trustee, reserving the right to specify a replacement if the first choice doesn't work out.

The problem: If the grantor can remove a trustee and appoint a successor, the IRS wants the replacement to be "independent" (and not a subordinate or relative of the creator). Otherwise, insurance proceeds still are subject to estate tax. Subordinates include employees of companies the insured controls (but not his or her partners). Relatives include spouse, parents, descendants, and siblings (but not nieces, nephews or in-laws).

My recommendation: If a creator can remove a trustee (and appoint a successor too), have the trust document specify that a new fiduciary cannot be the grantor's subordinate or relative.

MISTAKE # 12:

Forgetting to transfer existing policies to the ILIT. Usually, ILITs are established to own new policies. Unfortunately, it's easy to forget that old life insurance policies also should be owned by ILITs. Here are some suggestions:

·   Let's suppose there are two whole life policies (cash values $20,000 and $30,000). If you don't have enough Crummey withdrawal beneficiaries in one year, consider gifting these policies (one per year) over a 24 month period.

·   Perhaps you are insured under a group term policy. Before gifting it, make sure the master policy and your state's law permit this transfer. In calculating an annual gift, add the amount your employer contributes to your share of the premium. For example, the premium gift for a $500,000 policy—age 65 is probably about $25,000.

·   If you are qualifying gifts under Crummey withdrawal notices, keep in mind that term insurance has no cash values. Consequently, once a premium is paid, there is nothing for a beneficiary to withdraw. Consider giving the trustee an option to sell this policy to the insured for the value of the premium. By using this procedure, at least a beneficiary is assured of his or her cash if they want it.

CAUTION: Keep in mind always that it takes three years to remove a gifted policy from the transferor - insured's estate tax base.

MISTAKE # 13:

Transferring policies the "wrong" way. Every tax planning strategy seems to have one truly awful trap. ILITs are no exception. Be aware that when you transfer personal cash value policies to an ILIT, you can easily create an income tax problem for the trustee. Here's how:

Let's say there is a $500,000 whole life policy, and you've

paid $80,000 in premiums. The cash value is $100,000, and since you don't want to gift that much money to the trust, you borrow $90,000 from the policy before making the transfer. *The issue:* Is there a tax trap?

Yes! Since the loan ($90,000) exceeds premiums paid ($80,000), you'll pay an income tax at the point of transfer on $10,000 of profit. Since the trust assumes this loan (and interest payments), tax law then subjects the face amount to income tax at death. (This is a so-called transfer-for-value rule, and in this situation the trust pays income tax on the face amount—$500,000 less payment for the policy of $90,000—and less future premiums paid by the trust.)

Here's the *problem:* By borrowing more than premiums paid, an income tax issue is created for you and an enormous income tax issue is created for the trust. You can resolve this in the following ways: 1) Lawyers avoid transfer-for-value issues by constructing a legitimate business partnership before the transfer; an ILIT and the insureds become the partners.[8] 2) Sidestep the matter by limiting policy loans to premiums paid at date of transfer-$80,000 in the above situation. 3) Have the trust obtain a new policy; then surrender the existing contract—you'll avoid the three year rule and the cash is yours as well. Just make sure the new policy is available before you surrender the old one.

---

8 Then when a policy is transferred to a partnership of which the insured is a partner, there is no transfer-for-value problem. Internal Revenue Code, Sec. 101(a)(1)(B).

MISTAKE # 14.

An incorrect split-dollar plan. Whenever there is a sharing of policy benefits and premiums between two or more parties, this is a split-dollar plan. It should be considered, if your objective is maximum estate tax-free death benefits in exchange for low premium-gifts. However, if a split dollar plan isn't arranged properly, it may lead to a tax and financial disaster. Here's why:

Let's say your ILIT has a $2 million policy. The premium gift is $70,000, but there are only three Crummey withdrawal beneficiaries. This limits tax-free annual gifts to $30,000 (3 X $10,000). The gift tax answer may be a split-dollar plan between the ILIT and an outside person or party. For example:

	Premiums	1st Year Policy Share
Outsider	$40,000	$40,000
ILIT	30,000	1,960,000
	$70,000	$2,000,000

The result: By paying less than one-half of the premium ($30,000), this ILIT has most of the insurance benefit—a $1.96 million first-year share. A split-dollar plan creates enormous leverage, and it should be considered in any serious wealth preservation planning.

The problem: The outsider should not be you (the insured) or any corporation where you have over a 50 percent vote (unless this business has no rights under the split-dollar agreement, except repayment of its advances at death or when the split dollar plan is terminated). Know also that after say 8 or 10 years, a split-dollar plan may give your ILIT some of the policy's cash value. IRS says this policy equity is a gift by you, and where your corporation is the outsider you'll probably pay an extra income tax as well.

My recommendation: It is possible to create a split-dollar plan that optimizes ILIT benefits and minimizes tax exposure. This takes an experienced tax lawyer with an insurance background, or at least an insurance planner knowledgeable about the law. Obtain the best help possible. Don't waste your money on mediocre assistance.

MISTAKE # 15:

"Reciprocal" trust plans. It's not uncommon for lawyers to draft two ILITs (one for a husband and one for a wife) when doing tax liquidity planning for the family. *The result* is a tax disaster. Here's why:

Let's say you establish an ILIT for spouse and children. Your spouse then creates a second ILIT for you and children. Each trust owns insurance on the life of its grantor. *The problem:* The IRS "uncrosses" these ILITs and *includes each policy in the creator's estate tax base. My recommendation:* If you have this plan, see a good tax lawyer now. It's too late after someone dies. You may need to start over once more.

Observation: Perhaps you create an ILIT for a brother's family (and he does the same for you). These are also considered "reciprocal" trusts. Moreover, the story is the same even though neither your brother or you are trust beneficiaries.

MISTAKE # 16:

Not extending this trust when there is "danger." Earlier, I defined an ILIT "as a trust that terminates when the insured (and spouse) die." In other words, the trust distributes property to children outright when it's time for them to inherit. This can be a mistake, especially if a child is having legal or marital difficulties at that time.

As I mentioned in Chapter 8, a revocable living trust should be extended when a distribution of assets places them in jeopardy. An ILIT that terminates at death should also be extended under similar circumstances.

My recommendation: If your beneficiary is insolvent, bankrupt or experiencing financial difficulties, give your trustee authority to continue the ILIT until there is no more danger. If the beneficiary is trustee, provide that another trustee has responsibility for this decision.

This possibility of extending a trust share points out an advantage of extending trusts permanently. In Chapter 10, you'll learn how to extend trusts that shelter property for spouse and children. Chapter 11 will cover perpetual trusts, which are maintained for generations to come. If you feel strongly about preserving family wealth, you won't want to miss this information.

CHAPTER 10

EXTENDED TRUSTS:
AN RLT OR ILIT
CONTINUES FOR YOUR SPOUSE
AND FAMILY

I   In Chapter 8, I introduced the revocable living trust
    (RLT), and explained why it's the best way to main-
tain financial privacy, avoid probate, and manage your assets if you're disabled. In Chapter 9, I explained why an
irrevocable life insurance trust (ILIT) is the key to a good
tax liquidity plan. Well, if RLTs and ILITs are the "glue"
that hold an estate together, an *extended* trust is what protects assets for the next generation.

For our purposes, I'll define extended trusts as former
RLTs or ILITs created by someone who has died. The RLT
protected his or her assets, and the ILIT eliminated insurance proceeds from the estate tax base. An extended trust is
used to loan cash to, or acquire assets from, a personal representative, and maintain a fund for children until they die.
Then grandchildren receive trust assets outright. If there are
no grandchildren, everything is paid to siblings (or nieces

and nephews). Until distributed, trust shares are managed carefully and protected from a beneficiary's lawsuits, failed marriages and family conflict. Be aware, however, that at a child's death there is a flat 55 percent generation skipping transfer tax (GSTT) when assets pass to the next generation -your grandchildren[1]; or an estate tax (37 to 60 percent) if your child-beneficiary *virtually* owned a trust share. It depends on how the document is written. I'll explain which tax to pay in the pages ahead. For clarity, you might want to compare this definition to the definitions of revocable living trusts (Chapter 8) and irrevocable life insurance trusts (Chapter 9).

There are two ways to acquire wealth — earn it, or get it the "old fashioned way" by inheritance. When you receive gifts or bequests, they are either *direct* (outright) or *indirect* (in trust for your benefit). At first blush, you'd think outright ownership is better than having an interest in a trust fund. That's not true, but it's understandable to think that way. Frankly, it isn't the ownership itself you prefer, but what it *represents* - namely, rights to income; to select the investments or those who make the investment decisions; to use or consume principal, if necessary; and to have a say in where the money eventually goes (sales, gifts or bequests).

Experts say that outright ownership actually interferes with personal financial goals, however. Keep in mind that when you own something, anyone who covets it more can prob-

---

[1] Of course, it's possible to protect up to $1 million from GSTT, but for this chapter-I'll presume this amount is used to shelter *other* assets from the 55 percent tax. In chapter 11, *Perpetual Trusts,* I'll outline how to use this GSTT exemption.

ably get their hands on it. What you own is particularly vulnerable to lawsuits. And, since 55-60 percent of all marriages end in dissolution, chances are you'll end up in litigation at least once in your lifetime. What's worse, divorce court judges tend to toss all of the assets in a "pot" and divide them 50-50 anyway.

When there's a marital breakup, it's not unusual to incur some severe financial losses - even bankruptcy (and that's another lawsuit). There are also normal business and personal problems that could place you right in the middle of a flourishing U.S. legal system. If this isn't enough, malpractice claims can haunt lawyers, doctors and other professionals for their entire careers. Finally, the IRS may disagree with how you calculate income or transfer taxes and haul you into Tax Court. You just never know what's ahead.

Realistically, the property you *own* is always at risk in a complex society that wants what you have. Here's the bottom line: A well-conceived trust arrangement created by a considerate benefactor is always preferable to outright ownership. As trust beneficiary, you can *virtually* own everything; you needn't *actually* own it.

Indeed, for many decades, the wealthy have crafted trusts to keep family assets away from others who want the money.[2] It's just better to place all gifts and bequests to loved ones in trusts. Our legal system blesses these structures and encour-

---

2 For example, see *du Pont, (William),* Forbes 400, where there is a casual (but typical) comment that "impenetrable trusts safeguarded his (Henry Eleuthere Irenee's) inheritance from business losses"-Henry is William du Pont's grandchild.

ages their continuation. This brings us to the benefit of extending an RLT or ILIT for the use of others. But beware: There are still traps to avoid along the way. Let's examine them here:

***Trap #1: Not Having An Extended Trust.*.** Denver lawyer, Bruce Schilken, explains it this way. He helped a client establish an extended trust who was concerned about his son, Bill - a spendthrift in the true sense of the word. The trust creator died, and one day, Bill showed up driving a huge motorcycle. Bruce was immediately concerned that Bill would be upset with him for "locking up his inheritance."

To the contrary, Bill thanked Bruce for keeping the money protected. Due to his aggressive life-style, Bill feared that there wouldn't be anything left without the security of his trust. So, Bill has a monthly check mailed to his next port-of-call, and no one else can get their hands on his inheritance.

The next time you think about making an outright gift or bequest, remember how many Bills there are who don't have the slightest idea how to manage or keep money intact. You'd be amazed how many times estate documents leave everything directly to those who cannot hold onto a dollar bill. *My recommendation:* Create an RLT or ILIT that becomes an extended trust for your children. Make it flexible, and help them *control* rather than *own* their inherited property.

Trap #2: Keeping An Extended Trust In A "Pot." The first decision when designing an extended trust is whether to keep property in a "pot" for the entire family. Frankly, I prefer separate shares, hands down. Normally, everything is kept in a single "pot trust" to benefit all beneficiaries usually according to need) when there are one or two major holdings such as a family business or large real estate properties. This approach to trust management is convenient, and it offers the possibility that valuable family assets won't be fragmented and wasted in the process.

However, I generally recommend placing assets in separate trust funds for each beneficiary. For example, a child active in a family business receives voting stock in his or her share. An inactive child's share receives cash or insurance proceeds. If there isn't enough money, give the inactive child nonvoting stock that has a preference for dividends. Divide the real estate, but if it can't be split, set aside portions for everyone. Here's why it's best to have separate, equal trust shares.

My recommendation: Separate trust shares place each descending line on its own philosophically and financially. This approach enables children to know brothers, sisters, nieces, nephews and other relatives personally, without the crippling entanglements that only money can confer. It's just that simple.

Trap #3: Not Thinking "Maximum Benefits" For Beneficiaries. I'm still surprised most people think of trusts as "locking up" money where no one can get it. This is far from the truth. Trusts can be just as flexible as a creator wishes. All it takes is a good lawyer and some creative imagination.

If the goal is virtual ownership, I call this a "maximum benefits" trust. In this arrangement, a beneficiary may also be trustee with the right to control investments. He or she can also receive the income and have unlimited power to withdraw principal. Finally, a beneficiary can have complete authority over gifts and bequests of trust assets to others. This is called a power of appointment and is simply the right to designate who eventually receives trust assets.

Keep in mind that at a child's death, an extended trust is terminated and it pays a 55 percent GST tax or an estate tax on the value of assets transferred to grandchildren. Consequently, this trust can virtually be "owned" by children in the meantime. From a tax perspective, there is no difficulty giving them nearly as much power over an extended trust share as if they owned it themselves - it's taxed anyway when they die.

CAUTION: If a beneficiary can demand trust property, you can be sure that a mean-spirited creditor can probably force a trustee to pay out these funds from the trust. Therefore, a "maximum benefits" trust fund can be lost if there is a lawsuit. *My recommendation:* Although there is always room for a "maximum benefits" arrangement, a "management" trust does a much better job of preserving family wealth.

Trap #4: Not Thinking Management For Beneficiaries. Usually, asset management is the primary goal of an extended trust. The document grants a trustee specific authority to distribute funds in a complete range of investments. A disinterested or independent fiduciary (which need not be the investment or management trustee) distributes principal and income to a beneficiary, depending on his or her needs, and the trust builds up its remaining assets for the future. Although a management trust gives a beneficiary less than virtual ownership or maximum benefits, it can really come in handy in the right situation. Consider the following, which clearly illustrates a need for carefully arranged trust management:

A beneficiary becomes ill or has an automobile accident and is unable to handle personal affairs. *My recommendation:* If this is a maximum benefits trust, it should now become a "support" trust that provides management and flexibility for the disabled person. It might even be converted to a "luxury" trust that gives a level of benefits above those which social and government agencies typically offer. A luxury trust usually begins where society leaves off, and it also protects trust property until legitimate entitlements are spent to care for the incapacitated person.

Trap #5: Not Thinking "Asset Protection" For Beneficiaries. As mentioned, one of the problems with a maximum benefits trust is that a creditor may seek a force-out of distributions to the beneficiary. This makes it especially difficult to keep the trust fund intact.

CAUTION: A maximum benefits trust can be lost to creditors who obtain the property to satisfy claims. *My recommendation:* Whenever a beneficiary incurs financial difficulties or there is "danger," the trust should shift to a discretionary arrangement. Then, a disinterested trustee has sole authority to make distributions, but is specifically told not to pay funds to a creditor or prospective claimant. Most law honors these instructions, and an independent fiduciary will not be required to go against the creator's wishes.

Please take this matter of extended trusts seriously. Know whether your beneficiary is capable of managing money, or if he or she needs help with financial matters - you'll want to provide the proper balance in the document. As the creator, your extended trust can emphasize maximum benefits or asset management and protection. It depends on your point of view.

Trap #6: Not Choosing Trustees Wisely. A family member was probably trustee when your ILIT held only an insurance policy. But when a trust continues for the next generation, you must select a successor trustee. You might choose a friend, bank or trust company, or you may even put a beneficiary in charge. Let's look at the options:

· *A friend as trustee:* Consider the trust of Hugh F. Culverhouse, deceased former owner of the Tampa Bay Buccaneers. According to 1997 newspaper accounts, he selected three lawyer friends as trustee for his wife,[3] Joy Culverhouse. Liquid trust assets *increased* over about two years from $5 million to $80 million, and debts were *reduced* from $115 million to zero. However, Mrs. Culverhouse was upset about the trustees' fees which ran into the millions, and she sued

3 It may actually be unethical if the lawyer accepts employment as trustee or representative under your trust or will. The following is an ethical rule of thumb attributed to respected lawyer Floyd McGown of San Antonio, Texas. (As an attorney) "Do not accept service as a fiduciary in a trust or will created by a client."

to remove Hugh's friends from control. There was a lot of testimony about palimony and extramarital affairs, and the whole matter ended in the spring of 1997 when the trustees paid their legal fees of over $1 million *from the trust.* Sometimes you can't win; it seems to always be about money.[4]

·   A *professional trustee:* A bank or trust department offers neutrality, investment experience, and perpetual existence.[5] These are sound reasons to choose a professional trustee. In addition, when choosing a state's law to govern the trust, it may be necessary to have a corporate trustee in the state in order to connect with a particular jurisdiction.[6]

·   A *beneficiary-trustee:* Finally, it's possible to select a

4 See "Lawsuit to Open Against Trustees," Feb. 3, 1997, "Trustees Present Defense of Estate Work With Widow," February, 1997, Sarasota Charities, USF benefit from settlement, Feb. 7, 1997, and "Culverhouse Trust Fires Trustee," March, 1997;- all in the *Sarasota Herald-Tribune.*

5 Averell Harriman left his widow Pamela, more than $100 million and apparently designated her as an executor and trustee, also-See Marilyn Berger, "Pamela Harriman, Diplomat, Dies at 76," a *New York Times* feature published in *The Denver Post,* Feb. 6, 1997, p. 24A. Unfortunately, this started a family dispute. Pamela Harriman, the U.S. Ambassador to France, was sued in 1995 by Averell's heirs who claimed she participated in bad investments. See "Ambassador Sued Over Inheritance," *USA Today,* Oct. 19, 1995, p. 3A. This matter might have been softened if professional trustees were in charge instead of individuals. As they say, however, hindsight is always the best teacher. On the other hand, see "Georgia Sues Nationsbank Over Publisher's Estate," *The Wall Street Journal,* Sept. 17, 1997. This article describes a 1996 lawsuit where the State of Georgia claims a bank trustee failed to set up a charitable trust 51 years earlier in 1945. The will of W. T. Anderson mandated this trust benefit indigent blacks and allegedly, this professional trustee overlooked the details.

6 For example, Alaska has recently enacted laws that promise certain tax and creditor advantages for Alaskan trusts. The hitch: Unless you know someone in Alaska that can be your trustee, the fiduciary must be a trust company or bank that is located there. See Carolyn T. Geer, "Is Your Trust Well Placed," *Forbes* magazine, June 16, 1997, p. 190.

family beneficiary as trustee. The *advantages* are (a) less expense, (b) familiarity with the assets, and (c) knowledge of family values and philosophy. The possible *disadvantages* include (a) inexperience as fiduciaries, and (b) difficulties when there are disputes.

CAUTION: Unfortunately, most people aren't careful enough when choosing a trustee long term. It may simply be a bank where the family has a personal loan. *My recommendation:* Have a specific trustee strategy when a trust is continued beyond a creator's death. Let me give you a few helpful hints.

In general, trustees perform three functions: They keep records, invest the money, and make distributions to beneficiaries. Therefore, it's possible to have more than one fiduciary. Perhaps a bank does the paperwork and makes discretionary payments to beneficiaries, an "interested" beneficiary-trustee makes distributions required by the trust, and a third fiduciary invests the assets. Of course, several trustees can complicate the situation, and you must have legal papers drawn to protect everyone. I just mention this possibility to show what can be accomplished by a creative trustee arrangement.

Trusts are flexible, and they needn't tie everything up in knots. Think of trustees as managers - there can be one, two or three who are in charge. You can even change them later to suit your family's needs and circumstances over the years.

Let's look at a few more potential dangers with extended trusts:

Trap #7: The "Casual" Selection Of A Trust's Location. There is a paragraph (usually near the last page of a trust agreement) that normally names the creator's state of residence as the governing law for the trust. This can be a mistake - long range - because states differ when it comes to asset protection, income taxes, and even trust investing and accounting procedures. For instance, some states, like New York, may forbid changing a trust's "situs," even though the trustee and beneficiary have moved to another state.

Let's say you establish an ILIT in Iowa which taxes trust income, or Colorado which doesn't provide much creditor protection for insurance cash values. The beneficiaries might find it difficult to transfer the trust to South Dakota or Delaware, where there is no state income tax, or perhaps Texas which shelters all life insurance and annuity cash values from creditors. *My recommendation:* Give an independent trust protector authority to change location of the trust, and hope the original state okays this approach. Better yet: Carefully locate the trust in the right state in the first place.

Trap #8: No Trust Committee Or Protector. As I've mentioned, a trustee generally performs three functions (See Trap #6). It keeps records, chooses investments and makes distributions to the beneficiaries. Although trustees typically resist change, sometimes it's just in everyone's best interest to change location (even move the trust to a foreign country), choose another trustee, or amend or terminate the trust if it isn't working. A protector or trust committee handles these tasks, making any necessary modifications that are in the best interest of the beneficiaries. Think of a protector as having a single task – to assure the creator's wishes are fulfilled.

My recommendation: One approach to selecting a protector is to list several candidates in the trust when it's created. A beneficiary selects one of them and, perhaps, two or three successor candidates. When a protector dies or resigns, the beneficiary chooses another from the list, and a similar procedure continues until the trust is terminated.

Trap #9: Not Specifying A Spouse Spend Personal Assets Before "Family Trust" Assets Are Distributed. When an RLT or ILIT becomes an extended trust, there may be a surviving spouse as well as children. If so, the trust will likely be divided initially into two shares.

The first portion will be a "family trust" equal in value to the deceased's personal exemption, currently $600,000. (See Illustration #1.) Let's suppose this trust provides income for your spouse and children at your spouse's death. (There is *no* estate tax when your spouse dies.) Then, it continues in separate shares until your children die.

The second portion is a "QTIP marital trust" that must pay income at least annually to the surviving spouse. (There *is* an estate tax on these assets when your spouse dies.) At your spouse's death, this trust fund merges with assets of the family trust until the deaths of your children.

CAUTION: Usually, the family trust pays all income, as well as principal, to your spouse. Since your spouse may not need these funds, his or her estate tax base can be increased

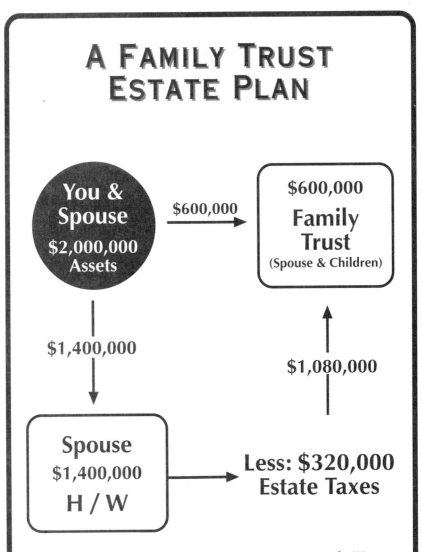

Illustration 1: By leaving $600,000 to a Family Trust, which children receive tax-free at the second death, you and your spouse obtain *two* $600,000 "exemptions" for your estates. Instead of paying $588,000, your children owe merely $320,000 in estate taxes– *a savings of $268,000!*

unnecessarily when these distributions are added to his or her other assets.

My recommendation: Have the family trust specify (in the absence of special circumstances) that no payments are made to your spouse until the marital trust has been spent or liquidated. By first spending down personal and marital trust property, the assets are removed from your spouse's estate tax base. At the same time, a family trust builds up its holdings for use at a later date. You might even think of this as a "take and put" financial and estate planning strategy.

Trap #10: No Discussion Of Incentives. Most trusts simply leave distributions up to the trustees. This gives substance to the notion that a child is a "trust fund baby," and sometimes he or she simply gets used to a regular trust income. *The result:* Some people think this prevents a child from developing independence.

My recommendation: If you feel that money can sometimes do more harm than good, consider language in an extended trust that gives children incentives to do good works. Here are a few examples:

A. Match (up to a limit) each dollar your child earns, and give the trustee discretion to pay out additional amounts of principal and income for health, education, maintenance and support (HEMS);

B. Make principal distributions tied to attaining a certain net worth;

C. Match each donation your child makes to charity;

D. Pay for your child's advanced education; and

E. Provide extra funds if your child enters a less than lucrative, but desirable career   such as a missionary, school teacher or social worker.

Let your imagination create incentives. Trusts needn't be "rubber stamp" boilerplate documents. Although some say that incentive trusts rule from the grave, I believe they offer opportunities for people to achieve meaningful goals in life – separate from money issues.

Trap # 11: Not Encouraging Unproductive Trust Assets For Use Of Beneficiaries. In 1997, a trust pays a high 39.6 percent tax rate on income over $8,100. Of course, if taxable income is paid to a beneficiary, this is a tax deduction to the trust and taxable income to the recipient.

CAUTION: When something is taxable, someone has to pay the tax - and it's usually at a high rate. *My recommendation:* Specifically, let the trust acquire non-income assets such as cash value life insurance, closely-held stock, family limited partnership units and vacation homes—or collectibles such as vintage automobiles, art, jewelry, or coins. Then, the trust leases the vacation home, art or jewelry at low or no rent. Under present law, it appears the value of this bargain isn't taxable.

By holding unproductive assets for the use of beneficiaries, neither trust nor recipient need worry about income taxes. Collectibles may also make good investments, and they enhance long-range growth potential for the trust. (Certainly, a Renoir or Van Gogh painting is attractive in the home, regardless of the owner - no one will ever know!)

Trap # 12: Excluding A Child's Spouse. A typical (child's) beneficiary clause reads something like this:

"From a trust share for a child of mine, my trustee shall make payments of principal and income for life. At a child's death, the assets shall be distributed to my grandchildren in equal shares."

CAUTION: This approach can make your grandchildren wealthy at the expense of their parents.

Let's suppose you leave your son $2 million in an extended trust, and he dies while married to Nancy. They have two children, Susan and Lynne, who are ages 15 and 7. Each daughter receives income from the trust fund, and principal is paid at age 21. For the rest of their lives, Susan and Lynne have more money than their mother. Meanwhile, Nancy may be forced to remarry or work in a part-time job, to maintain herself, even though she had wealthy in-laws.

My recommendation: Include trust language that provides for your child's spouse, at least until remarriage. One possibility is an annuity policy that pays a set income; another is a cash payment when the trust is terminated and grandchildren receive their shares.

Trap #13: No Power To Insure The Life Of A Beneficiary. We've defined an extended trust as ending at a child's death, when there is generation skipping transfer tax (GSTT) or estate tax to pay. ***CAUTION:*** The problem with this is that grandchildren must pay immense sums just to get an inheritance. *My recommendation:* Permit your child's trust to insure his or her life. This provides tax liquidity to protect your grandchildren. *Better yet:* Permit your child's trust to split-dollar a policy with an ILIT that your child creates. This way, the ILIT's death benefit share won't be part of an insured's taxable estate.

Let's say your son, Bill, creates an ILIT that acquires a $1 million policy on his life. The annual premium is $20,000. Using split dollar, Bill's personal ILIT pays a small premium share averaging $4,000 over the years, and his extended trust pays the premium balance. *The result:* The trust helps Bill create tax liquidity, but the insurance proceeds are mostly in his ILIT, where they are excluded from his estate tax base like the insurance at your death.

CAUTION: If Bill is also trustee of an extended trust, have a disinterested party make insurance decisions, or the IRS may include the ILIT's share of the proceeds in your son's estate tax base. (This issue is especially important when the extended trust becomes a perpetual trust—chapter 11, and the goal is to protect its assets from transfer taxes for generations to come.)

A COMPARISON OF THE GENERATION-SKIPPING TRANSFER TAX (GSTT) AND THE ESTATE AND GIFT TAX

One of the purposes of the U.S. transfer tax system is to assess a transfer excise tax whenever assets pass to anyone but a surviving spouse or charity. There is either an estate or gift tax, a generation skipping transfer tax (GSTT), or both.

Presently, gift and estate tax rates start after a $600,000 "exemption," at 37 percent. Then, they increase gradually to 60 percent for holdings between $10 million and $21.04 million. There is a 55 percent rate on assets over $21.04 million. (Bear in mind that I've assumed an extended trust is terminated when a child-beneficiary dies. If he or she has virtual ownership, there is an estate tax to pay.)

The GSTT works this way: It used to be possible for one generation after another to inherit in trust, without anyone paying a gift or estate tax along the way. These generation-skipping trusts became favorite strategies of the Vanderbilts, DuPonts, Kennedys and Rockefellers, but middle America wasn't especially fascinated with them until the 1970's and 1980's As I mentioned, when a child-beneficiary dies without virtual ownership in an extended trust share, there is a 55 percent GSTT.

In 1986, to halt perceived tax abuse, Congress enacted a flat 55 percent GSTT due whenever gifts or bequests skip an intervening generation.[7] For example, there is a GSTT when making a bequest directly to your grandchild. There is also a GSTT when your child's extended trust share passes to your grandchild (GC), or on distributions to future generations if everything continues after your child dies. Somehow, Congress wants to tax each group of descendants whether or not they actually transfer the wealth.

To make things simpler, let's assume you have a $2 million estate, and it pays a $1 million estate tax (at a 50 percent rate) at your death. $1 million net is available for descendants. Here are a few inheritance possibilities.

---

7 But *see* note 1, *supra.*

· *You make a bequest directly to your children.* There may be an estate tax when *they* die.

· *You make a bequest directly to your grandchildren.* They pay a GSTT of $354,938 [.55 x ($1,000,000 ^ 1.55)] at *your* death.

· *You arrange an extended trust for your children and then to your grandchildren outright.* When your grandchildren receive their inheritance, they may pay an estate tax, or a GSTT of $550,000. It all depends on the terms of the trust.

· *You arrange a perpetual trust for generations to come* (see chapter 11). A 55 percent GSTT is paid each time distributions are made to your grandchildren and future generations.

TRANSFER TAX PROBLEMS WHEN YOUR CHILDREN DIE

It's when an extended trust is *terminated,* and either a GSTT or an estate tax is due, dangers lurk. Here are a few:

Problem # 1. Paying A GSTT When There Should Be An Estate Tax. It certainly doesn't make sense to pay a GSTT if an estate tax amount is less.

If your son dies with an estate of under $3 million, where estate tax rates are less than a flat 55 percent, the estate tax should be paid. For instance, if his personal assets are nil, his estate would owe $153,000 in estate tax on a $1 million trust fund, but the trust would pay a whopping $550,000 if it owes a GSTT instead.

My recommendation: If an estate tax may be less expensive than a GSTT, have the trust document permit a trustee to give your child *virtual ownership,* such as the right to terminate the trust or make bequests of trust assets to his or her personal creditors. These powers place the trust fund in a beneficiary's estate tax base.

Problem # 2: Paying An Estate Tax When There Should Be A GSTT. It's possible that a 55 percent GSTT may actually be *less* than the estate tax. There can be state taxes that cause overall inheritance and estate taxes to exceed 55 percent, or your child may have a personal estate of over $10 million where the estate tax rate is 60 percent.

My recommendation: In these circumstances, caution the trustee not to give your child *virtual* ownership in the trust fund. Just pay the 55 percent GSTT - it will cost less.

Problem # 3: Paying An Estate Tax When There Shouldn't Be Any. While an extended trust normally passes outright to your grandchild, your child could die childless. In this circumstance, your child's trust fund may pass to a sibling or parent. If there is no grandchild or great grandchild to receive the trust share, there can be no GSTT.

For instance, your son dies without a child or grandchild, and his trust fund passes directly to his sister. ***CAUTION:*** There is no GSTT, but if trust documents give him virtual ownership along the way, his sister pays *unnecessary* estate taxes.

My recommendation: In situations where there may be no lineal descendants, make sure the trust document avoids giving your child the virtual ownership that places it in his or her estate tax base. Otherwise, someone pays a needless estate tax.

Trap #14: Failing To Extend This Trust When There Is Danger. As I mentioned in Chapters 8 and 9, it's wise to extend an RLT or ILIT when there is danger.

CAUTION: Even with an extended trust, there is always a possibility that your grandchildren will receive their shares at a time when there's danger or they just aren't mature enough to handle the money.

My recommendation: If your grandchildren are insolvent, bankrupt or experiencing difficulties, give your trustee authority to continue an extended trust until the danger has passed. *Better yet:* Create a trust that is extended perpetually for generations to come. You'll learn more about these in Chapter 11.

In summary, an extended trust is an RLT or ILIT that continues for one generation, and then, the assets are usually paid to your grandchildren. It either emphasizes maximum benefits or management, or it shifts from one philosophy to another, depending upon the requirements of its beneficiaries. At your child's death, this trust pays estate taxes where a beneficiary has virtual ownership, a GSTT tax where there is no virtual ownership, or neither tax when assets pass to siblings or ancestors.

CHAPTER 11

PERPETUAL TRUSTS:
AN ILIT EXTENDED TRUST ENDURES FOR GENERATIONS TO COME

I n Chapter 10, I described how an extended trust continues after its creator dies, providing for spouse and children (until their deaths). During this time, it's managed carefully to protect assets from lawsuits, failed marriages and family conflict. If this arrangement is maintained for generations to come, it becomes a *perpetual* trust - the cornerstone of all wealth preservation planning. I'll discuss the perpetual trust (which is sometimes referred to as a "dynasty" or "generation-skipping" trust) in this chapter.

For our purposes, let's define a perpetual trust as once having been an extended trust (see Chapter 10); however, its assets aren't paid over to grandchildren when children die. Instead, it continues for future generations. It's possible for beneficiaries to control shares of a perpetual trust, but they don't virtually own them. Consequently, there are never estate taxes to pay. Since a grantor's $1 million generation-skipping transfer tax (GSTT) exemption is carefully allocated to gifts and bequests to this trust, there is no 55 percent GSTT to pay either, as each generation benefits from this arrangement. For clarity, I suggest that you compare this definition to the definition of revocable trusts in Chapter 8, irrevocable life insurance trusts in Chapter 9, and extended trusts in Chapter 10.

Once you use the $1 million exemption to protect a perpetual trust, the trustee, as well as the trust document, must avoid situations where a trust share is virtually owned by the beneficiary and unintentionally included in his or her estate tax base. I'll explain how to give a beneficiary incidental or indirect control, instead, without "upgrading" this to the ownership that attracts an estate tax. Here's a brief refresher.

Remember, as I told you in Chapter 10, that tax advisors routinely created perpetual trusts for the Vanderbilts, Kennedys, Rockefellers and DuPonts earlier in the 20th century. Congress finally took notice and actually enacted a generation-skipping transfer tax (GSTT) law in 1976; in 1986, this legislation was repealed and a new law set in place a flat 55 percent GS tax. This 1986 law is currently in effect in 1997. Although middle America is now more aware of GS planning, these arrangements haven't been the same since the 1986 law was signed.

If the 55 percent GS tax eventually traps assets in trusts, why all of the emphasis on perpetual trusts? When this law was enacted, Congress also granted each taxpayer a $1 million GS exemption. You can dedicate this amount to protect gifts, bequests, or both. It's your choice.

Imagine that! After paying a gift or estate tax, it's possible to transfer up to $1 million that keeps providing for your family - possibly forever. If you make a bequest, the exempt limit is truly $1 million. If, however, you leverage this exemption now by making gifts, the protected amount by your death may be far greater than $1 million.

Now for the real tax magic: By creating a perpetual trust that acquires life insurance, beneficiaries are assured a GS trust that is much larger than $1 million. And this sum is promised as soon as the policy is approved.

Let's say you and spouse are in your 50s You have extra funds and want to take advantage of two $1 million GS exemptions. You contribute $80,000 annually for 25 years (until age 80) to an ILIT where the trustee acquires a $10 million last survivor life insurance policy. (At age 65, you might acquire a $10 million policy with annual premium gifts of about $135,000 for 15 years - a total of about $2 million - until age 80.)

The result: At most, you commit $2 million financially to a perpetual trust that is worth $10 million for your children, grandchildren, and future generations. And, if the trust is managed properly, they won't pay a GS tax or an estate tax as trust assets pass from one beneficiary to another.

CAUTION: Your attorney must prepare a perpetual trust carefully. If the plan doesn't work well, your grandchildren and future generations will have to pay a 55 percent GS tax on each dollar taken in the future. It's necessary, therefore, to avoid mistakes when so much is at stake.

Let's talk about what can go wrong with perpetual trusts. I suggest you read this material twice. If it's still unclear to you, take it to a tax advisor (or call me with your questions). Be aware that the law can change this opportunity at any time.

POTENTIAL PROBLEMS WITH PERPETUAL TRUSTS

PROBLEM # 1.

Not Having A Perpetual Trust. All wealth preservation strategies have disadvantages, and perpetual trusts are no exception. There are even some myths that have been circulated over the years that we need to discuss. Consider these popular notions about long range GS planning:

Myth #1: "I don't want to skip over my children to my grandchildren." You can always include children in a GS trust. And they can have a significant economic interest as well in its assets. Here are a few rights and powers you can give all beneficiaries without ever subjecting their trust shares to gift, estate or GS taxes.

· They can withdraw all trust income, or 5 percent of trust principal annually, or additional principal for health, education, maintenance and support (HEMS).

CAUTION: In Chapter 10, I explained that if a beneficiary is entitled to income and principal, a creditor may force out these payments. Therefore, it's usually better to make a beneficiary merely eligible for these sums. For example, in-

stead of mandatory payouts, a trustee-beneficiary has discretionary authority to make distributions for health, education, maintenance and support. If danger arises, this trustee
resigns and gives his or her authority to an independent party
— perhaps a friend.

· They can be trustee of their own separate GS trust;

· An independent or disinterested trustee can pay them
income and principal for any reason;

· They can remove an independent trustee and name a
successor;

· They can manage the trust's investments;

· They can give or bequeath (appoint) assets to friends
and family; and

· With built-in "trap doors" (see Chapter 9), they can
participate in the termination of their GS trust (if ever there's
some reason to do this).

Note: When a beneficiary dies, his or her separate GS trust
may be divided into new separate trusts for grandchildren,
great-grandchildren, etc., with similar benefits provided for
them.

Again, the tax law allows each beneficiary these financial
benefits without anyone paying a GS tax or an estate tax
along the way. In addition, there are some intriguing non-
tax reasons for choosing perpetual trusts. For example:

· Beneficiaries can refer investment salespeople to their
trustee;

· If there is a lawsuit, marital breakup or family
squabble, a perpetual trust is secure and safe from those who

want its assets; and

There is no need to worry about estate liquidity because this trust reaches the next generation free of taxes, worry, and probate.

Myth #2: "I don't want to tie everything up." As I've suggested, perpetual trusts can be quite flexible. Moreover, sometimes it's just best to keep everything in trust. Consider the will of Martha Frick Symington, the mother of former Arizona Governor Fife Symington. Mrs. Symington died in November of 1996, about 14 months after her son filed bankruptcy. According to the *Arizona Republic,* she left a perpetual trust that provided that a number of paintings be managed for her son's benefit.[1] (This is probably a classic arrangement that permits a trustee to use unproductive assets for the use of the beneficiary.) Apparently, Mrs. Symington also intended to protect her son's inheritance from his creditors, and I predict this will be accomplished.

Myth #3: "I can 'only' leave them #1 million." Of course, you can't protect more than $1 million in a bequest to a perpetual trust. However, this amount can be leveraged by using a gifting approach. An ILIT is an alternative when GS gifts are made early and often. That's why most tax professionals suggest lifetime perpetual trusts, as I have defined them.

Myth #4: "What if everything goes wrong?" A well-crafted perpetual trust should always have trap doors for ben-

---

1 Jerry Kammer, "Mother Left No Cash for Symington," *The Arizona Republic,* Jan., 1997, p. A1.

eficiaries (as I describe them for trust creators in Chapter 9). These permit everyone to cancel their trust if it isn't working. As mentioned, it's much easier to terminate a trust than it is to start a wealth preservation plan from scratch.

Myth #5: "**What happens if they change the law?**" It's always possible that Congress may change the estate or GS tax law. For example, let's imagine that the $1 million exemption limit is reduced to $500,000, or even eliminated for future GS transfers. Gifts already made are grandfathered and protected.[2] That's another reason why I favor starting a perpetual trust now.

Myth #6: "A perpetual trust is more expensive." That's probably true. Since it will last for many years, your attorney will take longer to prepare an ILIT; naturally, this increases the cost. But, everything considered, it's well worth this expense.

The bottom line is that you and your family can't lose with a perpetual trust. Yet, only a fraction of all family wealth continues in trust for even one generation (see Extended Trusts Chapter 10). As described in Chapter 9, most trusts are terminated when the creator dies.

Let's turn our attention now to other potential problems with a perpetual trust:

---

2 See Thomas M. Forrest, "Dynasty Trusts: A Powerful Estate Planning Tool," *National Association of Estate Planners & Councils*, Winter 1996, p. 4, where the author reminds us that Congress has power to charge the law regarding perpetual trusts by enacting a "federal rule against perpetuities." In other words, it's better to create one of these trusts now when the law in somewhat lax.

PROBLEM # 2.

Not Having A Specific Gift-Giving Strategy. When the plan is to make lifetime gifts to a perpetual trust, it makes sense to have a good gift-giving strategy. Otherwise, you aren't taking full advantage of the law. Below are some possibilities. In each situation, your accountant claims against your GS exemption on a Form 709 gift tax return when you file your income tax return:

Example #1: *You gift $10,000 annually to a Crummey withdrawal ILIT (Chapter 9) for your two sons, and the trustee purchases an insurance policy.*

CAUTION: Notice that I suggested gifts that total $10,000 for your two sons, and not $10,000 per child. There are some complicated rules if gifts to a perpetual trust are more than $5,000 per child. Keep matters simple; limit annual gifts to $5,000 when using Crummey withdrawal perpetual trusts.

Example #2: *You gift $50,000 each year to an ILIT that is not a Crummey withdrawal trust. Eventually, you pay gift taxes when your total gifting exceeds $600,000.*

Example #3: *You gift $1 million to an ILIT now, and pay a gift tax of $153,000 on $400,000 after claiming the $600,000 gift tax "exemption."*

In each of these examples, it's possible to gift extra amounts and claim a spouse's exemptions also, if you're married and your spouse consents to the plan.

PROBLEM # 3:

Failing To Allocate The $1 Million GS Exemption. It's possible to establish a perpetual trust with the best of intentions, and simply forget to claim your GS tax exemption. For instance, you establish an ILIT and make gifts to the trust. However, the responsibility for filing a gift tax return Form 709 and allocating the exemption isn't acknowledged. In other words, the job doesn't get done, and the trust isn't fully protected from the GS tax.

My recommendation: Acquaint your tax preparer with the plan, and provide gift premium payment information to make sure gift tax Form 709 is filed annually with income tax Form 1040. Then elect to use portions of your GS exemption on this form until your full $1 million is claimed.

PROBLEM # 4:

No Maximum Rule Against Perpetuities (RAP) Period. The $1 million exemption protects contributions and the ultimate value of these funds from future transfer taxes. But how long these funds remain in a perpetual trust depends on the rules of the state that govern your trust. Usually, this is a flat 90 years or a period measured by the rule against perpetuities (RAP). A RAP period commences on the date an ILIT is created, and continues until after the last deaths of individuals specified in the trust, plus 21 years. The problem is that most GS trusts aren't set up to last very long. *My recommendation:* Learn how long a perpetual trust can continue, and create an arrangement that lasts as long as possible.

Let's suppose you create an ILIT today and specify that it will last for the RAP period in your state. The "measuring lives" are your son, age 40, and grandson, age 10. This trust should last until 21 years after the death of your grandson. (If he dies in 70 years at age 80, the trust lasts 91 years.)[3] Then, it's possible for an independent trustee to skip over your great grandchildren (GGC) all the way to a younger descendant - perhaps even a great-great-great-great grandchild in his or her formative years. This strategy can keep the trust fund away from the GS tax and estate taxes for 150 years or more!

Of course, a perpetual trust lasts indefinitely. Presently, at least five states (and several foreign jurisdictions as well) don't have a RAP. These are Delaware, Idaho, Alaska, South Dakota and Wisconsin, and other states are also considering a "no-limit" RAP. In these locations, perpetual trusts can conceivably avoid U.S. transfer taxes forever.

CAUTION: If you choose South Dakota or Delaware (where there is also no trust income tax) as the situs of a trust, a lawyer will probably advise that at least one trustee live there. And it will not be possible to include out-of-state real estate in this trust, unless land is placed in a partnership or corporation whose shares are located in South Dakota.

PROBLEM # 5:

Disregarding A Spouse's $1 Million GS Exemption. If

---

[3]For a comprehensive example of the rule against perpetuities, see Richard W. Duff, *Preserving Family Wealth Using Tax Magic, Strategies Worth Millions,* (Berkley, 1995), pp. 133-144.

you own most of your family's assets, you may be wasting your spouse's $1 million GS exemption. Let's assume you have a $2 million estate and your spouse has none. You wish to protect this entire amount from transfer taxes for generations to come. If you're the first to die, your lawyer must craft estate documents carefully to qualify $1 million each for the exemption. However, if your spouse dies first, it will not be possible to protect more than your $1 million exemption.

My recommendation: When you own most of the family's assets, you can split gifts with your spouse and allocate some of his or her exemption when making lifetime gifts. Then, a creative set of estate documents bequeaths any unused balance.

For example: You purchase a large insurance policy in an ILIT; the annual premium is $80,000. After 10 years, you and your spouse die in a car accident, and each of you have claimed $400,000 of a $1 million GS exemption—a total of $800,000. If you've also split the remaining $1.2 million of family assets, your wills each leave $600,000 to this trust by bequest. The result: You protect two $1 million GS exemptions, instead of one.

PROBLEM # 6:

Omitting A "Family Bank" Strategy. Traditionally, trusts are supposed to invest in income-producing assets and make cash distributions to its beneficiaries. Indeed, volumes are written about situations where trustees didn't earn enough income to suit the expensive tastes of their recipients. Actually, a "maximum income" payout strategy is probably a mistake for a perpetual trust. When it comes to truly preserving family assets, a perpetual trust accomplishes this by providing "the use of" assets instead of income and cash flow from investments.

Example #1: A $1 million trust fund earns income of $80,000 each year. When this is distributed, the beneficiary has $48,000 (60 percent) after paying income taxes of $32,000 (40 percent). This "build-up" in the beneficiary's name is available immediately to taxes, lawsuits and the possibility of a failed marriage. If instead, funds remain in the trust, they are usually sheltered much better from those who want them.

Example #2: A trust fund doesn't invest in income-producing assets. Instead, it leases a home for its beneficiary rent-free. There are no income tax consequences to the trust or the beneficiary, and the home appreciates in the trust for future generations, without ever paying transfer taxes.

Example #3: A trust fund acquires collectibles - jewelry, art, heirlooms and coins — that are leased rent-free for the enjoyment of each generation.

Example #4: A trust fund makes business loans and scholarships available to beneficiaries at minimum interest rates. Eligibility for the funds is determined by the trust document.

My recommendation: Once more, instead of distributing taxable funds to someone, a perpetual trust acquires assets for "the use and enjoyment of" a beneficiary. This approach enables the trust to maintain protected capital and avoid most income taxes in the meantime. What an intriguing method of preserving family wealth!

PROBLEM # 7:

Creating An Estate Tax By Allowing A Beneficiary To Withdraw For Pleasure, Happiness Or Comfort. Beneficiaries can withdraw trust assets for health, education, maintenance and support (HEMS) without including trust shares in their estate tax base. (Or, as interested trustees, they can take HEMS payments personally.) If this perpetual trust is protected by allocation of the $1 million exemption to gifts and bequests, there is no 55 percent GS tax.

CAUTION: Let's suppose a trust permits the beneficiary to take payments for happiness, pleasure or comfort. In the law, these words are considered vague and the same as virtual ownership. Thus, when a beneficiary dies, the trust fund becomes part of his or her estate tax base.

My recommendation: Permit only independent disinterested trustees to make distributions for happiness, pleasure or comfort. If a beneficiary or beneficiary-trustee can demand principal, you should limit distributions for HEMS only.

PROBLEM # 8:

Creating An Estate Tax By Allowing A Beneficiary Funds That Can Satisfy An Obligation To Support. If a trust requires an interested trustee to distribute trust funds for the support of a beneficiary's dependents, the IRS may place the trust assets in the beneficiary's estate tax base. Why? Since parents have a legal obligation to support children, they actually become the children's creditors. And when funds are made available to pay someone's debts, they are included in the estate tax base.

My recommendation: Even though this trust fund is protected from the 55 percent GS tax, it's best to specify that the trust cannot distribute funds to satisfy a beneficiary's obligation of support.

PROBLEM # 9:

Creating An Estate Tax By Giving A Beneficiary Too Much Control Over Removing Trustees And Choosing A Replacement. Over the "life" of a perpetual trust, it's natural to anticipate a regular turnover of trustees. A beneficiary moves to another state, and asks a professional trustee to resign, a friend-trustee dies or resigns, or a beneficiary-trustee dies or becomes disabled, and the next generation must step into the role of fiduciary. The law is concerned about who names the replacement and who has the power to remove a trustee. If a mistake is made here, there will most certainly be a tax disaster.

Let's suppose a disinterested professional trustee can distribute principal for any reason. A beneficiary can remove this trustee and select a favorite relative or subordinate as a replacement. *CAUTION:* This is more than control - it is virtual ownership - and trust assets are then included in this beneficiary's estate tax base.

My recommendation: Where a beneficiary can remove an independent trustee who has full authority over distributions, restrict the choice of successor to an independent fiduciary. Otherwise, the beneficiary has virtual ownership over his or her trust fund share.

Some good news: If an existing trustee's authority over distributions is limited to HEMS, apparently a beneficiary can remove a trustee and name anyone as a replacement without attracting estate taxes. Also, if a trustee voluntarily resigns, a beneficiary can appoint any successor if permitted by the trust document.

PROBLEM # 10:

Not Specifying That A Beneficiary Spend Personal Assets Before Trust Assets Are Distributed. Technically, a trust can pay to a beneficiary all income, as well as additional principal. But this well-meaning language can "leak" assets to someone who might not need them.

Let's say your son, Bill, is beneficiary of a $2 million perpetual trust. He earns $100,000 annually, and at the moment, this is sufficient for his needs. However, his trust also has investment income of $100,000, which is paid to him whether he needs it or not. *CAUTION:* Unfortunately, Bill must reinvest the trust payment, and this gradually creates a significant estate tax base in his name.

My recommendation: Have the trust accumulate income for Bill's use at a later date, which will not increase his estate tax base unnecessarily. As long as his trust holds this income, it can also be sheltered from judgment creditors, a failed marriage or a family conflict. It's just better to keep assets in a "rainy day" trust until they are needed. Better yet: Let the trustee acquire unproductive assets and make them available for Bill's use. This way, there is neither trust income or an income tax .

PROBLEM # 11:

The 37 1/2 Year "Trap." In general, your lineal descendants are classified as "non-skip" persons (children) and "skip" persons (grandchildren or more remote descendants). Strangers or friends born more than 37½ years after your birth are also "skip" persons. When it comes to these non-relatives, even experts can fall into a GS trap.

There's a story about an 80-year old Chicago lawyer who left a large estate to his mistress, age 40. You can imagine her surprise when she had to pay both an estate tax (no marital deduction) and a 55 percent GS tax after his death. *My recommendation:* Well … I'll leave this one up to you.

PROBLEM # 12:

Mixing "Exempt" with "Non-Exempt" Trust Assets. Sometimes a perpetual trust receives gifts and bequests of more than $1 million. If so, a portion of each distribution is tax-free, and a 55 percent tax is incurred on the remainder of the payment. This can create unnecessary taxes and confusion for the "life" of the trust.

For instance, an ILIT has a $2 million policy, and the premiums until your death are $500,000. You protect these premiums from GS tax by claiming exemptions on a gift tax return Form 709 when premium gifts are made. Eventually, your will bequeaths an extra $1 million to this trust. The total contributions to the trust, therefore, are $1.5 million (instead of the protected $1 million limit). *CAUTION:* Whenever the trustee pays funds to your grandchildren (and more remote descendants) only ⅔ of each distribution is protected from a GS tax. Your trustee will have some complicated record-keeping ahead.

My recommendation: When it's possible a perpetual trust will receive more than $1 million, leave the excess to a separate non-exempt trust. Then, treat the non-exempt trust as an extended trust, which pays GS tax or estate taxes when assets pass to descendants, and no estate taxes when they are distributed to brothers and sisters (see Chapter 10).

PROBLEM #13:

Placing hard-to-value assets in a perpetual trust. I've mentioned that when more than $1 million is placed in a "dynasty" trust, there is a 55 percent GS tax on a portion of each payment to a "skip" person (your grandchildren, great grandchildren, etc.) Whenever hard-to-value assets are contributed to a GS trust, they may create this same problem.

CAUTION: You contribute real estate of $1 million to a GS trust, but the IRS claims this gift is really worth $2 million. A court settles the matter for a value of $1.5 million. Therefore, when your grandchildren receive distributions, ⅔ is free of a GS tax, but there is tax on ⅓ of each payment. This can cause significant administrative confusion.

My recommendation: Limit GS trust contributions to easily valued investments. Cash, treasuries, marketable securities and mutual funds are probably best. To be safe, limit the transfers to less than $1 million.

PROBLEM #14:

Avoiding Vested Trusts. When you make a $10,000 gift to a trust for a grandchild or great grandchild only, the law exempts this transfer from a GS tax. *CAUTION:* The rules require that a trust's assets must eventually vest and become part of the descendant's estate tax base at death.

My recommendation: You can gift $10,000 to a vested trust for your grandchild and not use your $1 million GS exemption to protect it. This trust can leverage your gift by insuring the life of your grandchild, his or her spouse, a parent or even a grandparent. Keep in mind, however, that this isn't a perpetual trust that continues for future generations. Rather, it ceases at your grandchild's death.

Once established, you can add your spouse's $10,000 to this trust annually, and other family members can also contribute $10,000. By encouraging additional gifts, your grandchild may have a substantial kitty someday that comes in handy for education or retirement.

PROBLEM #15:

Not Leveraging A Perpetual Trust With Life Insurance. In this chapter, I refer to a perpetual ILIT. Of course, it's not necessary that a trust begin as a life insurance trust; it's just better if it does.

For example: You begin a gift giving plan to a perpetual trust, created to last for generations to come, and you want it to begin now to accumulate much more than $1 million by your death.

The best investments for perpetual trusts are assets that have good growth possibilities. [4] Life insurance is an excellent choice because it truly "explodes" in value at a specific moment in time. This feature increases the value of the proceeds significantly, and they are also income tax-free. Once established, all perpetual trusts should own property that has good growth potential; life insurance just makes this accumulation predictable.

PROBLEM # 16:

No Charitable "Gift Over" At Termination. It's always possible that a perpetual trust will terminate because there are no more descendants. *CAUTION:* The state then receives trust assets (by the process of escheat) when they could pass to charity.

My recommendation: Have the trust document provide a charitable "gift over" whenever there are no more heirs.

In summary, a perpetual trust is an extended ILIT that continues for generations to come because the creator's $1 million GS exemption is allocated to gifts and bequests made to the trust. Its assets and trust distributions are exempt from

4 Las Vegas lawyer Dick Oshins suggests an "opportunity shifting" trust. For example, you establish a perpetual trust for a spouse. A trustee acquires minority shares in a new business venture owned by the family. Eventually, the trust sells its shares at a considerable profit, and everything "explodes" in a perpetual trust for the benefit of generations to come.

the 55 percent GS tax, and the trust is crafted carefully not to give beneficiaries virtual ownership along the way. When this is accomplished, estate taxes are also avoided and you've created a private "dynasty" (in your name) for family, charity or friends — the penultimate wealth preservation plan.

AFTERWORD

Now that you've completed this book, you know what's required to fail-safe your estate plan. But understanding, alone, is not enough. If you're not a professional planner, you'll probably need expert assistance to execute these ideas. This book was never meant to substitute for the counsel of professional planners (although it may help keep them on their toes!)

If you need information about the services offered by CFPs, CLUs, CPAs, ChFCs, and how to get the best help for your particular circumstances, write to me for a free brochure. I can also send you information on organizations that make available the best articles, books and pamphlets on all wealth preservation topics.

If you're unsure about how estate planners work, let me share with you the philosophy I've come to over the years. From my point of view, the best *estate advisors* are more concerned with educating their clients than whether they are paid too much or too little. They keep up-to-date about new ideas and enjoy the opportunity to attend quality continuing education seminars. They share their ideas with other professionals, perhaps serving as speakers in their industry Finally, they know that wealth preservation is a team effort and enjoy working with other co-professionals.

Estate owners can contribute to the quality of this relationship –and the final result– by taking responsibility for their personal financial and estate planning. Good estate owners are pro-active. They may attend seminars and community presentations to learn more about these subjects. They seek out the best planners and are willing to pay for quality. And while they expect the best, and more, they are tolerant in those rare instances when things go wrong.) Pro-active estate owners also keep their estate plans up-to-date and share concerns with family members. They request input from children and relatives about their views and philosophy. And they willingly refer colleagues and friends to advisors who are interested in up-to-date thinking. The world of business turns on relationships. The more you serve them, the better they serve you.

INDEX

Perelman, Ronald 32
Perpetual Trusts 250, 252, 273,
    274, 277, 278, 279, 280,
    281, 283, 292
personal representative 84, 93, 104,
    105, 218, 227, 232, 251
phantom income 200
Picasso, Pablo 11, 206
Pot Trust 254, 255
power to change trustees 245
pre 59 1/2 10 percent penalty tax
    166
pre 59 1/2 excise tax 158
Premium Payments 186
Preserving Family Wealth 12, 283
Presley, Deborah Delaine 214
Presley, Elvis 214
Presley, Lisa Marie 214
primary beneficiary 160
Princess Grace of Monaco 202
probate 25, 40, 149, 160, 161,
    162, 163, 189, 195, 217,
    220, 221, 222, 223, 224,
    251, 279
protector 234, 262, 263
provisional income 149
Pulitzer, Joseph 225

Q

QDOT 44, 45, 195
QP 71, 74, 75, 76, 79, 81, 83,
    84, 85, 86, 87, 88
QP account
    74, 75, 79, 84, 85, 86, 88
QP Tax Liquidity 84
QTIP Trust 87
Quaker State Refining Corporation
    217
qualified domestic trust 44, 195

R

RAP period 282
recalculation 80, 81, 85
"reciprocal" trusts 249
retirement income 64, 69,
    70, 71, 91
revocable living trust 17, 122, 123,
    162, 202, 218, 222, 250,
    251, 252
Ritchey, Eleanor 217
Ritter, Bob 117
RLT 123, 162, 202, 219,
    220, 221, 222, 224, 225,
    251, 255, 263, 272
Robbie, Joe 39
Rockefellers 269, 274
rollover
    73, 82, 84, 85, 86, 87, 88
Roth IRA 74
Roth, Sen. William 74

S

Saunders, Katherine 225
Schilken, Bruce 255
SCIN 59, 60
Second Marriages 42
"Sell" Strategy 57
Separate trust shares 256
Seven Deadly Mistakes 70
Shrinking Gift Property 108
Sikes Corporation 60
Sikes, Jimmy 60
Sikes, Leon 61
Simmons, Harold 106
Simpson, O. J. 75
situs 262, 283
Social Security benefits 149
Sotheby's 121
Sovereign Trust 223
"Spigot" NIMCRUT 130
split dollar 56, 142, 248, 249, 268

THE AUTHOR

Richard W. Duff, J. D., CLU, is a financial planner, consultant and the author of *Preserving Family Wealth Using Tax Magic - Strategies Worth Millions!* (Berkley Books, N.Y., 1995). This consumer-friendly book caters to middle and upper income taxpayers. It clearly explains the legal/financial vehicles and concepts that add up to substantial tax-savings at death. Numerous examples, charts and illustrations make the information easy to follow. *Preserving Family Wealth* and *Keep Every Last Dime* draw from the strategies Dick has used successfully with his clients for over 32 years.

Well-known as a leader in inheritance planning across the country, Dick has earned lifetime membership in the Million Dollar Round Table. He is also a six-time qualifier of the Top of the Table. A popular speaker at industry gatherings and consultant to top financial planners, he advises his peers on how to preserve their clients' assets. His consulting extends to writing columns for such respected publications as *Broker World* and *The Journal of Financial Planning*. He has also contributed book chapters on wealth preservation and financial planning to anthologies published by Dearborn Press, which has compiled the writing of the top experts in this field.

Mr. Duff considers it his mission to educate audiences about how to protect their hard-earned wealth and provide for their families and favorite philanthropies. He has done more than perhaps any other financial planning expert to demystify financial planning for the lay reader.

Mr. Duff makes his home in Denver. He is a 1965 graduate of the University of Iowa Law School, and has a bachelor's degree in marketing.